Charles Somerville Latrobe Bateman

The First Ascent of the Kasaï

Being some records of service under the Lone Star

Charles Somerville Latrobe Bateman

The First Ascent of the Kasaï
Being some records of service under the Lone Star

ISBN/EAN: 9783337037192

Printed in Europe, USA, Canada, Australia, Japan

Cover: Foto ©ninafisch / pixelio.de

More available books at **www.hansebooks.com**

THE
FIRST ASCENT OF THE KASAÏ:

BEING SOME RECORDS OF SERVICE

UNDER THE LONE STAR.

BY

CHARLES SOMERVILLE LATROBE BATEMAN,

SOMETIME CAPTAIN AND ADJUTANT OF GENDARMERIE IN
THE CONGO FREE STATE.

*WITH FIFTY-SEVEN ILLUSTRATIONS AND TWO MAPS REPRODUCED
FROM THE AUTHOR'S ORIGINAL DRAWINGS.*

NEW YORK:
DODD, MEAD & COMPANY,
753 AND 755 BROADWAY.
1889.

TO

H. B.

IN GRATEFUL ACKNOWLEDGMENT OF MUCH GENEROUS
SYMPATHY AND HELP

This Work

IS AFFECTIONATELY INSCRIBED

BY HER NEPHEW

THE AUTHOR

PREFACE.

AT a time when so many narratives of African travel, adventure, and discovery are before the reading world, the appearance of a new volume, which must be classed with works of that description, undoubtedly demands some few words of apology and introduction.

It is necessary, therefore, for me to explain that the following narrative, forming, in point of fact, a monograph on the Bashilangé-Baluba nation, is the record of my later experiences in the service of the Congo State: a service which I had entered shortly before the A.I.A. obtained full political recognition in its consolidated form as the Free State of the Congo.

Were my object in making public any portion of my African life merely the gratification of the love of adventure or of the marvellous, or were it the exhibition of myself as an actor in scenes of tragic incident, I should have selected for publication the story of the first few months of my service under the State. But although the object of this work precludes my giving the detail of those occurrences, yet, as they introduced me to the country and the life I am about to describe, I feel that at least the outline of them, so far as it shapes my story, must be presented to my readers.

For several years previous to my engagement with the State, I had resided on the south-west coast of Africa, chiefly at Mayumba, where I represented a Liverpool trading firm, and was consequently prepared for many of the difficulties with which, on accepting service early in 1884 under Captain Grant-Elliott, I almost immediately found myself environed. These difficulties were occasioned mainly by the presence upon the coast of an European and semi-European population of mixed nationality but almost unmixed villainy: a population consisting for the most part of Portuguese criminals and British outcasts, with a fair sprinkling of unfortunate people of various nations and all ranks. Their entire immunity from all control of law, the license of their lives, and their relations with the natives, naturally disposed them against the introduction of anything resembling regular government, and the circumstances of the inevitable collision with these people are indelibly burnt into my memory. I began my work at Mayumba by annexing to the then Kwilo Province of the State (since ceded to France) the country in the immediate neighbourhood, and thereafter proceeding to the Upper Nyanga, concluded in that hitherto unexplored district treaties of annexation with the chiefs.

Appointed in July 1884 to the adjutancy of gendarmerie at Grantville, I saw some active service in troubles arising from the conflict of jurisdiction between the French and Congo authorities, and, in company with the late Lieut. Hurt, R.N., made a complete route survey of the country between the Mayumba lagoon and the Kwilo-Niadi at Franktown, the chief features of which have become known to the public, and are incorporated in the most recent maps. After moving to Massabé in the November following, I was appointed (on the cession of the Kwilo Province) to the adjutancy of the camp of instruction then in course of formation at Lutété, in the basin of the Lower Congo. It was while I was in command there that Dr. Wolf arrived, having left at Léopoldville the main body of Lieut. Wissmann's expedition. At Lutété he met Sir Francis de Winton, K.C.M.G., at that time commanding the Province, and as a result of their meeting I was despatched under Dr. Wolf's command in charge of the Bashilangé-Baluba auxiliaries of the German expedition on their return to their own country: the narrative of which return and its immediate sequel form the subject-matter of these pages.

Doubtless the chief claim to novelty and interest that my little work may be held to possess is a superficial one, and lies in the fact that it is less a record of discovery than of life in a newly discovered land, and is a fair illustration of the *raison d'être* and practical working of the Congo State. But in transcribing the bare jottings of my diary have had more than one object in view—aims which sharply differentiate my work from those of African travellers properly so called, and which constitute the best apology for its existence.

I have, in the first place, wished, without being tiresomely statistical and technical, to give, in the broad interests of science, as exact and lively a representation of places and things, climate, scenery, and people, as my ability allowed; and to achieve this end the better, I have been careful to describe as best I might, not merely the outward appearance of things, but the impression produced on my own mind and heart by the circumstances occurring around me and by the scenery through which I passed.

In the next place, in the interests of trade, as well as of my class, I have endeavoured to make my remarks as to house-building, planting, and some few processes, game and hunting, and administrative and military routine, as full, explicit, and practical as without prolixity I could.

In the cause of humanity and philanthropy, of the missionary and honest trader, I have endeavoured to expose the covert slave-trade carried on by the Angolese subjects of Portugal. It is, however, but right that I should draw attention to the difference existing between slave-owning and slave-dealing. So far as I can see, slavery must exist in the regions watered by the Congo and its tributaries for a very long period to come: its suppression, were it possible, would lead to anarchy and misery without conceivable limits. But slave-dealing is quite another matter, and it is practically suppressed in the limits of the Congo State, except where, at its east and north-eastern extremity, the Arab invasion carries with it the curses of murder, misery, and devastation. In the same interests, too, I devote considerable space to the description of several interesting races in addition to the Bashilangé-Baluba, and have given accounts more or less minute of such singular characters as Chilunga Meso, and of such organisations of evil as the Lubuku brotherhood.

I have ventured thus to point out the practical value I have sought to impart to the following narrative, because works of the kind are too apt to be looked upon as entertaining reading merely, and where they fail to amuse they fail altogether. I wish to amuse, but I wish also to instruct.

I have viewed the story, too, as a portion of my own experiences: it is but fair that I should note that it is possessed of a much higher claim to public attention. It gives in a succinct form no inconsiderable section of the discoveries of the German expedition under Lieut. Wissmann and Dr. Wolf, in which the paths of other explorers, Livingstone and Cameron, Stanley and others, are crossed and united.

I have but few literary or artistic obligations to acknowledge, but I have to thank Lieut. Massari of the Royal Italian Navy for the gift of a rough chart of the lower portion of the Kasaï, which has been of service to me. My eldest brother, the Rev. J. H. Latrobe Bateman, has acted as my amanuensis throughout, and has undertaken the superintendence of my work in the press. I trust I have not misrepresented the opinions of any traveller, but I must confess that to arrive at an exact estimate of their precise scope and value has not been in every instance an easy task.

In conclusion, I have to observe that there is one subject conspicuous by its almost entire absence from my narrative: I allude to the progress of religious effort in ameliorating the social and intellectual condition of the people. For my own part, although a member of the Church of England, I am content to view religion as a personal rather than an ecclesiastical question, and can be perfectly, and, shall I say? cheaply, tolerant of all who dissent from that form to which I from habitude assent. Had I therefore seen anything that interested me or struck me as being specially hopeful in the composition or conduct of the Baptist and other Reformed Missions in the State, I would gladly have recorded it; but I did not. Beyond Mr. Darling's (Baptist) devotion to his work, and his extreme kindness to me when I was ill and helpless, and the existence of the Baptist missionary steamer *Peace*—an admirable boat, which they contrived to launch on the Upper Congo for a tithe of what the *Stanley* cost—I saw nothing that calls for comment or acknowledgment. I would not, however, be misunderstood on this point. An earnest pioneer of religion has a much better chance in his isolation

PREFACE.

of acting also as a pioneer of civilisation than has the secular trader. I state that which is within my own experience, when I say that whenever an European is settled amongst savages one of two processes immediately begins: either he raises them towards his level or they drag him down to theirs. The European is constantly confronted with the cheapness and utter insecurity of human life on the one hand, while on the other he observes the ease with which the means of living and of merely animal gratification are obtained. To live—eating, drinking, sleeping, becomes to him the whole of life; it unconsciously sinks into his heart that nothing higher need be thought of, and if he looks around on what, so far, the introduction of government stations and the like has done for the negro, he is encouraged to ask indeed *cui bono?* But a religious missionary has at all events within himself the ever-abiding conviction that—

> "'Tis not the whole of life to live,
> Nor all of death to die."

C. S. LATROBE BATEMAN.

CARLISLE, *January* 1889.

NOTE ON THE ILLUSTRATIONS.

THE whole of the Illustrations are produced from the Author's original sketches in pencil, water-colour, pen and ink, or sepia, either made on the spot, or from views finished at leisure from rapidly drawn outlines accompanied by written directions entered in his sketch-book: none are derived directly or indirectly from photographs; the photographic apparatus belonging to the expedition having become useless during transit. The principal sketches—originally made in pencil or sepia—are represented in this work by six etchings, whose beauty has been greatly enhanced by the exquisite art and skill displayed in the process by Mr. S. Myers (a fact which the Author desires here gratefully to acknowledge), while five water-colours have been most carefully printed as nearly as possible in the original colours: the engraved vignettes, &c., represent indiscriminately sketches originally made in colour and in black and white, but are much reduced in size. With regard to the view of Léopoldville, the Author desires to remark that it represents *exactly* that station as it appeared when the expedition started for the Kasaï in 1885: it has since been very greatly changed.

CONTENTS.

	PAGE
THE PREFACE	vii
NOTE ON THE ILLUSTRATIONS	xiv
THE ARGUMENT	1

CHAPTER I.

The *personnel* of the party—Stanley Pool described—Start from Kinchasa—Wrecked—Wretched night and day—Recriminations—Nocturnal alarm—We contrive to communicate with Léopoldville—Repairs—The fresh start—The skipper's parrot—Congo scenery—The tropical forest—Msuata . 3

CHAPTER II.

Kwamouth and the Kwa—Narrative of Wissmann's discovery and descent of the Kasaï—The Baluba and their neighbours—Our departure—Scenery on the Kwa—Deserted Wabuma village and heronry—Castellated rocks—The Musjie villages and their Queen—The Nzali Mpini—Woodcutting—The Kwango 15

CHAPTER III.

Huts at Bosjie—River nomenclature—Forest villages and market-places—Excellent native iron-work—Mount Poggé—Probable embouchure of the Lukenyé—Curious huts—Timidity of inhabitants—An uncomfortable night—Hippopotami, buffaloes, and cowbirds—Accident to the *Stanley*—Hostility of Basongo-Meno—Their towns and punishment—A jovial chief—Repairs to *Stanley*—The expedition nearly blown up—The Luangi—An unknown tribe—A night upon the river 31

CONTENTS.

CHAPTER IV.

PAGE

The Sankoro—River nomenclature again discussed—The relative magnitude of the Sankoro and the Kasaï—A picnic—Aquatic birds—Bakuba country reached—A theft and quarrel—The *En Avant* constantly aground—Price of provisions—Friendly natives—The Lulua described—Its fish and fishermen—The end of our voyage 50

CHAPTER V.

Luebo—Its environs and our neighbours—The station site—Departure of the *Stanley*—The log-house—Calemba leaves for Kashia-Calemba followed by Dr. Wolf—Clearing, levelling, and building—Kassengé and its plantations—Habits and customs of the Bakèté—Their preparations of tobacco and cassava—Christmas festivities—Daily routine in station—My hospitalities—Sunday in Central Africa—Return of Dr. Wolf for the New Year—His departure in *En Avant* for further exploration of Sankoro—Tragic death of native girl 63

CHAPTER VI.

Portuguese traders—Senhores Saturnino, Carvalho, y Custodio—Their history and trade—Custodio's advice to Dr. Poggé—Carvalho's letter—The partner's application at Luebo—Saturnino and the Zingas—The dispute arranged—Zingas and their country—Progress of the station buildings—The Krupp howitzer—Dr. Wolf's return and the results of his voyage—An agreeable (?) surprise 81

CHAPTER VII.

Dr. Wolf attempts to ascend the Kasaï—The *En Avant* disabled—A perilous project—The *Peace* arrives with Lieut. Wissmann on board, and departs towing the *En Avant* down to Léopoldville—Vander Felson's farewell—Wissmann and Wolf go to Luluaburg, and thereafter explore the Kasaï up to its first falls—The *Stanley* arrives at Luebo—Adventure of the Baron de Schwerin—Results of Messrs. Wissmann and Wolf's excursion to the Kasaï—Our journey to Luluaburg—The neighbouring natives—Incidents of the march—Accident at the Miaw—Luluaburg—Congolemosch—Kashia-Calemba and the King—Lubuku and lhiamba-smoking 99

CHAPTER VIII.

Chilunga Meso and his visions—The burning brandy—Senhor Caxavalla—His friendship with Chilunga Meso—Kasongo and the embassy from Ulungu—My return to Luebo—General description of the route—Dumba—Landslip—Beni-Mnamba—Midnight alarm and Limo's bravery—Silence in the sunshine—Night in the forest—Awkward situation at Beni-Kashia—Arrival at Luebo 117

CHAPTER IX.

Senhor Carvalho's administration—The plantations and our crops—Misunderstanding with the Bakuba—Our Bakètè allies—Fireworks—Boat accident to Bakètè hunters on the Luebo—Ingratitude—Luebo Falls—Bakètè hunting-parties—Game of district—Slave-dealers 139

CHAPTER X.

Visit to Lukenga Manena—My namesake—Dishonesty of Jaô Domingos—Expedition against Biombé—Temporary imprisonment of the chief—Ground-nut oil—Carvalho's boat-building and project—Arrival of the *Stanley* with my successor—The Sanford expedition—I leave Luebo—Accident to the *Stanley*—Sacred island of Kimeh—Kwamouth and the Catholic Mission—The Abbé Krafft—Kinchasa and Léopoldville once more . . . 158

APPENDIX . 175

INDEX . 187

ILLUSTRATIONS.

CHROMO-LITHOGRAPHS.

I. The Southern Shore of Stanley Pool	.	*Frontispiece*
II. Fisherman of the Lulua	to face page	50
III. On the Road to Kassèngé .	,,	63
IV. The Homage of Congolemosch	,,	99
V. Luebo Station	,,	158

ETCHINGS.

VI. Léopoldville in 1885	to face page	1
VII. The Expedition Steamers at Kwamouth .	,,	15
VIII. Mount Poggé . .	,,	31
IX. The First Rapids on the Lulua .	,,	81
X. Chinyampobo from Luluaburg .	,,	117
XI. The Eastern Falls of the Luebo	,,	139

FULL-PAGE ENGRAVINGS.

XII. Kinchasa	to face page	3
XIII. Lulua Fish . . .	,,	59
XIV. Bakuba Cups and Knives . .	,,	97
XV. Looking Back Across the Musisi Valley .	,,	106
XVI. Luluaburg	,,	109
XVII. Landslip at Beni-Muamba	,,	128

SMALLER ENGRAVINGS.

	PAGE
1. "Dover Cliffs" . .	3
2. At the Gates of the Pool	6
3. A Musjie Village .	15
4. A Bashilangé Woman	20
5. A Chiplumba Man wearing Matchioko Head-dress	21
6. A Chiplumba Woman . . .	21
7. Wabuma Fishing-town and Heroury	26
8. Hut near Mount Poggé .	31
9. Huts at Bosjie-Massari .	32
10. Basongo-Meno Woman .	43
11. Basongo-Meno Implements .	44
12. Basongo-Meno Youth . .	46
13. Basongo-Meno Market-woman	48
14. Shammatuka Fishing-huts	50
15. Hippopotamus Trap	53
16. Bakuba Head-dress . .	54
17. The Lulua Rapids from the Station	60
18. In Kassèngé Village	63
19. The Log-house . .	65
20. A Bakèté Girl	68
21. A Bakèté Man	69
22. Pounding Cassava .	71
23. Kafinga—a Portrait	79
24. Zingas . .	81
25. Chitabo on Miaw . .	99
26. Lhiamba (*Cannabis Indica*) .	113
27. Beni-Ndumba .	117
28. Kasongo—a Portrait . .	124
29. Senhora Caxavalla—a Portrait	125

ILLUSTRATIONS.

SMALLER ENGRAVINGS—*Continued.*

		PAGE
30.	Lianas at Beni-Kashia .	134
31.	Tévivé (*Gossypium*)	137
32.	Bakèté Chiefs .	139
33.	Mpondé (*Sorghum*)	141
34.	Mpindé nguba (*Arachis*)	142
35.	Bakèté Hunters . .	148
36.	The Western Falls of the Luebo .	151
37.	Bambangala . .	154
38.	Ant-bear and Ant-hill .	156
39.	Ground-nut Oil-making .	158
40.	Kallina Point .	174

MAPS.

LUEBO STATION	*facing page*	64
GENERAL MAP SHOWING AUTHOR'S ROUTES (*folded*)	,,	186

Leopoldville in 1885.

ARGUMENT.

WHEN Stanley discovered the Upper Congo, in his great expedition through the Dark Continent, he carefully watched for the embouchures of any rivers flowing from the south which might be identified as the outlets of those great waters which Livingstone had discovered, and made known to the world as the Sankoro and Kasaï. These outlets Stanley believed he had found in the Lubiranzi, a magnificent river which pours its flood into the Congo no great distance below the Stanley Falls, and the Uruki, a stream joining the Congo through a very wide embouchure at Equator. Subsequently, having discovered the Kwa or Kwamuni, as the lower waters of the Kasaï were then exclusively known, and voyaging up it, and by the Nzali Mpini to Lake Léopold II., but neglecting to explore the infinitely greater stream coming from the opposite direction, he concluded that the waters of the Kwamuni were mainly derived from the lake, and that no other really great rivers entered the Congo from the south. This view being taken as ascertained fact, the questions which suggested themselves to geographers were, where do the waters of the Kasaï and Sankoro empty themselves if not by the Lubiranzi and Uruki? or, do they lose themselves in some inland sea or marsh? To solve this problem Lieutenant Wissmann was despatched by the Geographical Society of Berlin, and under special commission of the King of the Belgians. In a previous journey across Africa, in conjunction with Dr. Poggé, Lieutenant Wissmann had crossed the Upper Kasaï, and had experienced the friendly character of the natives in its vicinity. He now conceived the happy idea of entering the country from the province of Malange in Angola, and making overland to the head-waters of the Kasaï, to obtain there the assistance of the natives, and thence to descend the river to whatever bourne its course might carry him. His project was completely successful: he met with the most cordial and efficient assistance at the hands of Calemba, the intelligent and noble-minded king of the Baluba, who personally and together with a sufficient force of warriors embarked upon the waters of the Kasaï, to share whatever vicissitudes and dangers might await his guest in sailing down them to their ultimate and unknown goal. In due course the expedition reached the Congo, and proceeding to Léopoldville, were there received by Mr. Troup, in the absence of Captain Saulez. Thus his immediate object accomplished, Lieutenant Wissmann returned to Europe, leaving the further conduct of the expedition to Dr. Wolf. Under his charge the king, Calemba, and the faithful Baluba, were now to be escorted on their return home up the Kasaï, whither it was determined to send on the expedition, with the view of establishing a station at the confluence of the Lulua with the Luebo, as a port for the station of Luluaburg, founded by Lieutenant Wissmann when in the Baluba country, and left by him in charge of Mr. Bugslag. I was permitted to accompany this expedition as second in command. The stern-wheel steamer *Stanley* and the steam-launch *En Avant*, together with a large whaleboat, were to convey the Baluba and members of the expedition to their destination. The ascent of the Kasaï and the subsequent establishment of Luebo station form the subject of the following narrative.

KINCHASA   [*To face page 3.*]

"DOVER CLIFFS."

UNDER THE LONE STAR.

CHAPTER I.

The *personnel* of the party—Stanley Pool described—Start from Kinchasa—Wrecked—Wretched night and day—Recriminations—Nocturnal alarm—We contrive to communicate with Léopoldville—Repairs—The fresh start—The skipper's parrot—Congo scenery—The tropical forest—Msuata.

On the morning of the 30th of September 1885, soon after 7 A.M., I went on board the *En Avant*, then lying off the landing-place at Kinchasa. We had on board fifteen Zanzibaris and Angolese, three Baluba, and my two servants.* Mr. Vander Felson had charge of the navigation of the vessel, and Mr. Walker was the engineer. The

* Vide Appendix A.

Stanley, having on board the main body of the expedition, under command of Dr. Wolf, was to follow us a few days later from Léopoldville, which is distant some six miles from Kinchasa, and is at the extreme end coastwards of the navigation of the Middle and Upper Congo, which, at the point immediately beyond that station, plunges down the Livingstone Falls in awful and indescribable grandeur —for well nigh 200 miles a frightful descent of cataracts and rapids infinitely the wildest and grandest in all the world. The *En Avant* was to precede the *Stanley* as her *avant courier*, but, as things turned out, this detail of our operations had to be abandoned. Owing to the large number of persons, including women and children belonging to the Baluba, whom the steamers had to convey, it was necessary for us every night to find some suitable camping-ground whereon our living freight might find sleeping quarters. The king, Calemba, and Sir F. de Winton, K.C.M.G., who accompanied the expedition, though not in command, were also accommodated on board the *Stanley*, which carried Lieut. Andersson of the Royal Swedish Navy as her captain, with Mr. Olsen as mate, Mr. Waal as engineer, and Mr. Schneider as armourer.

Stanley Pool, upon which we were now embarked, is a singular feature of the Congo, which, for great distances both above and below this remarkable expansion, is, for so vast a river, decidedly narrow. The Pool is 20 miles long, and 16 miles broad in its widest part, being much blocked with sandbanks and islands, of which Bamu is the largest, measuring some $12\tfrac{1}{2}$ miles by $2\tfrac{1}{2}$ in its extreme length and breadth. The depth is very various, but attains a maximum of as much as 50 fathoms. The surface of the water is 910 feet over sea-level, and the banks are more or less elevated except on the southern shore. To the north-west the ground rises into hills, which display towards the Pool those strangely white cliffs nicknamed "Dover Cliffs." At "the Gates of the Pool," as the point at which the upper river begins to expand is called, both banks consist of bold hills rising about 600 feet over the water, clothed with wood at the base: those on the south side gradually retreating from the water, and sinking in height, until, behind Kinchasa, they disappear. To return, however, to the voyage before us. Unmooring at about 7.45 A.M. from Kinchasa, conspicuous on the low-lying shore by reason of its great baobab trees, we turned the prow of our boat against the stream, and steaming along the southern side of the Pool, we passed Kimpoko, where the American Methodist Mission is now located, at about 2 P.M., and encamped some two hours before sunset at the Gates of the Pool. Wood suitable for fuel being both good and abundant at this point, I kept the men cutting it until 10 P.M. Next morning, October 1st, having shipped the wood, we left our camp at 6.25 A.M. and proceeded on our way, keeping to the south bank, and with considerable difficulty contrived for some time to avoid the numerous reefs of rock; but having lost steerage-way in a whirlpool, we struck upon a rock some eighty yards from shore. As the steamer immediately began to fill, we beached her upon the nearest strip of sandy shore, but only just in time to save her, for the water was already lapping over into the engine compartment when we reached the bank. We proceeded to lighten the vessel by removing the wood, anchor, and anchor chain, &c., from the forward compartment to the land, and afterwards, having partially stopped the leak under her forefoot by letting down a weighted sail on that side of the bows which was exposed to the descending current of the river, we managed, with the assistance of a block and tackle fixed to a stout tree on the bank, so to

AT THE GATES OF THE POOL.

raise her fore part as to enable the engineer to ascertain the extent of the damage. This was considerable. There were four holes, one of triangular shape measuring three inches across the base, the others being smaller. Unhappily, the material of the steamer being steel, we could do nothing but await relief from Léopoldville, for in the turmoil of embarkation the drills, rivets, spare plates, and other requisites for executing repairs, had been left behind. Our situation was most unfortunate. Had the whaleboat been with us, or had we been provided with a row-boat of any description, we should have been able to communicate with Léopoldville. As things were, we could only wait upon our fortune. But we felt somewhat impatient, for we were threatened with a famine. We had fully expected to have reached Msuata on the following day, and had laid in no provision for a longer period, whilst the seemingly pathless forest by which we were surrounded forbade us to expect the presence of any native towns in our vicinity. Night closing in, I pitched my tent on a small open space of rising ground, Messrs. Vander Felson and Walker remaining on board the steamer, where they were sufficiently uncomfortable, and, I believe, mutually recriminative as to their several responsibilities in respect of our mishap. Next day our consultation was inevitably somewhat gloomy, but we decided on sending out two search-parties, I conducting one directly away from the river to look out for tracks or towns, Mr. Walker going with another along the river-bank in search of landing-places or canoes. Mr. Vander Felson remained in charge of the steamer and camp, with orders to hail any passing canoes, and to detain them until my return, so that I might have the opportunity of inducing their crews, either by bribes or threats, to convey intelligence of our disaster to Kinchasa or Léopoldville. After some hours of unsuccessful search, my party returned into camp, whither Mr. Walker had preceded us, and with no better fortune. The possibility of our provisions becoming exhausted did not tend to raise our spirits, and as we had to pass another night in our castaway condition, the feelings of my subordinates became yet more exacerbated towards each other. Indeed, their time on board must have been very trying to them that night, for, to the discomforts of their surroundings, were added the terrors of a threatened danger. Their rest was rudely disturbed by the grunting of a hippopotamus, who came about the landing-place in search of food. Our friends awoke at once to a sense of their new peril, and to a keener realisation of their former differences of opinion. Of course they differed as to the means and method of defence, and nature of the foe. They were in total darkness, and unable to procure a light. They stumbled and fell, and trampled on each other in their efforts to obtain their arms, and—I am afraid—they swore. Meanwhile the enemy retreated from the contest. On the 3rd of October we were so fortunate as to stop a passing Bayanzi canoe, bound for Kimpoko, with ivory, and induced them, by promises of reward, to take a letter to Kinchasa. Later in the day, two of the crew who had been sent out with guns to procure game of some kind, wherewith to supplement our scanty rations, came across a native road, by following which they arrived at a cluster of villages inhabited by a portion of the Batòkè tribe. These people proved very friendly, and promising to bring supplies into camp, the joyful return of our two men was speedily followed by the advent of a host of women with cassava, yams, fowls, plantains, &c.

The pleasing prospect of present abundance and coming escape so engrossed my mutually hostile companions that they forgot their past recriminations, and although the

HELP FROM LEOPOLDVILLE.

speedy discovery of the native road by the two Zanzibaris had to my mind, I must own, given confirmation to the reproach with which Mr. Vander Felson had assailed Mr. Walker as to the utter unreality of the latter's search for a landing-place, yet they now became and afterwards remained good friends and allies in their work. I passed the following day chiefly in shooting, and in considerably greater comfort. About 4 P.M. we were all gladdened by hearing the puffing and working of a steamboat coming up the river, and shortly after we had the pleasure of seeing the *Royal*, with Mr. Hamburg, engineer, on board, sent by Sir F. de Winton, in reply to my note, nearing the scene of our disaster. She brought with her all requisites for repairing the leak, and some comforts for the officers. The evening was spent more amicably than our previous evenings had been, and next day (October 5th) the united skill and industry of our engineers availed to make good the greatest part of the damage.

On the 6th of October both engineers fell early to their work, and repairs being completed, about 9 A.M. we pushed off the steamer into deep water, and commenced to reload. At 10 A.M. the *Stanley*, with the main body of the expedition on board, anchored off the landing-place. Dr. Wolf came on shore to receive my report, and with him were Sir F. de Winton, Dr. Leslie, Mr. Swinburne, and Mr. Troup—the two last-named gentlemen returning in the *Royal*. After half an hour's delay the *Stanley* proceeded on her voyage to Kwamouth, leaving orders that we should follow as soon as possible. The disaster which had befallen us was indicative of the part the *En Avant* was to bear thereafter in the expedition. We, who ought to have preceded the *Stanley* throughout the whole voyage for the purpose of securing a sufficiency of supplies along the proposed route, were generally following her, struggling vainly with our inferior engines against the current, or grounded on sandbanks.

All being ready for departure, we unmoored about 2 P.M. and proceeded up the stream. Crossing to the western shore, we were at some disadvantage from the heavy sea occasioned by the strong south-west wind meeting the current of the river. I confess that I was somewhat anxious myself as to the security of the repairs, but Mr. Vander Felson was afraid, distrusting an engineer's abilities to do anything aright, and his solicitude threatened to disturb his renewed friendship with the engineer. Between the whistling of the wind and the straining of the engine, it was no easy matter for him to make Mr. Walker, as he stood behind the funnel, hear his inquiries, or even to attract his attention. Grasping a yam, the worthy skipper watched for the opportunity that any change in Mr. Walker's position might afford him. After a time the engineer unsuspectingly ventured beyond his cover, when instantly the tuber went flying past his ear, and striking with force unlucky Mr. Vander Felson's favourite parrot, hurled it screaming into the eddies far astern.

"Hullo there! you've missed the pigeon, but you've killed the crow!"

"Oh, save my parrot!"

"Jump overboard, man, and save it yourself!"

"Stop the steamer! Stop her!"

"I'll do no such thing—stop the steamer yourself."

The parrot being abandoned to its fate, the skipper renewed the subject of the repairs, attracting the engineer's attention by an intermittent shower of various missiles.

"Is there any water there?"

"Yes, plenty."

"Does it increase, think you?"

"Yes; it's increasing fast enough."

"Ach Himmel! I knew it was so. We shall then all go to the bottom! Ach mine Gott! look now again and tell me is it so?"

"I'll tell you no more. Just you mind your own business and leave me to mind mine."

"It will be better on the other side. We shall cross the river."

"All right! that *is* your business—cross away!"

And so they kept on until the deepening shadows of the evening brought our voyage to a temporary close. We moored off a swampy strip of land on the northern bank. Here my tent was pitched, fires lighted, and the evening tasks allotted to all our little company. Although the lost parrot still formed the text of an occasional jeremiad, our social circle was more cheerful than the trials and controversies of the day would have justified us in anticipating. The next day our voyage was entirely uneventful so far as our progress was concerned, and at its close we encamped on the north bank, opposite to, though slightly below, Msuata.

The scenery through which we had passed since leaving the Pool is in many respects most beautiful, but, like the scenery elsewhere in this vast continent, it seems perhaps less beautiful than in reality it is: a fact, if fact it be, that I can only ascribe to the power of association to impress the mind. The broad level of the river gives contrast and relief to the bare bold hills through which its great path is cleft—hills which, though little varied by cliff and crag, and of somewhat uniform height, are garlanded and gemmed with all the dark luxuriant richness of the tropic forest and gilded with the most glorious sunshine. From the cool grey and gold of dawn on through the burning brilliance of the day to the rose and amber splendours of the sunset, the voyager may watch the nearing and receding bluffs with the fringe of forest round their bases, sometimes mirrored in the glassy stream and sometimes dimmed with haze or chequered with the fleeting cloud, but *lonely always:* unjoined with human story and the endless life of man. At home the records of our past, our glories and our griefs, from the remotest memories of the race, live in the features of the land; but in the country of an unknown past, through which the mighty river flows, the thought is borne ever onwards to a future no less unknown.*

The ground on which we were now encamped was high above the water, and grassy, but surrounded, save on the side next the river, by a dense forest. Although from sheer strength and luxuriance of growth the forests of Central Africa are of darker colour, and therefore a less attractive and showy element in the landscape, than forests are wont to be, yet it were a mistake to suppose that they are of one uniform dark evergreen tint. There are many trees whose

* Vide Appendix B.

tender green foliage contrasts finely with that of their darker neighbours; for example, the bombax or floss-wood, and the climbing calamus. There is also the beautiful traveller's tree, with its resplendent crimson foliage and silvery bark. There are, moreover, several flowering trees of great beauty; amongst them more than one species of acacia, and a magnolia with great creamy blossoms and delicious perfume.* The beach beside our camping-ground was very deeply marked with the spoor of elephants, buffalo, and various kinds of antelopes; but except a single specimen of the latter, a small blue buck that I shot before dinner, we saw nothing of the game. Next morning we left about 7 A.M., and keeping for a short distance to the north shore, soon crossed to the deserted station, but still considerable native towns, of Msuata. A station had been founded here by order of Mr. Stanley in 1882 by Lieut. Janssen, as a depôt for provisions and fuel for vessels ascending the river. Lieut. Janssen was much liked and respected by the natives, who were, so long as he lived, entirely friendly and well disposed; but after his lamented death—he was accidentally drowned, together with a French missionary priest, in the vicinity of the station — little misunderstandings induced coldness, which culminated in hostility. The ground on which the station was relinquished, however, was mainly the imperative necessity that arose, after Stanley's discovery of Lake Léopold II., of establishing a station at Kwamouth. The garrison therefore and *matériel* at Msuata was eventually removed thither, and our only object in landing at the old station site was to appropriate, for fuel, whatever might

* Vide Appendix C.

remain of the wooden buildings. Our task fulfilled, we turned away once more upon our upward voyage, and reached Kwamouth without further adventure of any kind at 4.30 P.M., where we found the *Stanley* already arrived before us.

A MUSJIE VILLAGE.

CHAPTER II.

Kwamouth and the Kwa—Narrative of Wissmann's discovery and descent of the Kasa—The Baluba and their neighbours—Our departure—Scenery on the Kwa—Deserted Wabuma village and heronry—Castellated rocks—The Musjie villages and their queen—The Nzali Mpini—Wood-cutting—The Kwango.

KWAMOUTH, as its name implies, is situated at the junction of the Kwa with the Congo, at this point about two miles wide, and flowing almost due north and south. The Kwa enters the main stream from the north-east—a swift river and very deep, but not much above 400 yards in width where it joins the Congo. The right, or Uyanzi, bank of the Kwa is bare and grassy, rising very gradually to a height of 200 feet and upwards. Opposite the ground rises steeply from the shore to an average altitude of 60 feet, forming thence, for some distance inland, a low plain, behind which the ground again rises. The station is located exactly at the embouchure and on the brink of this rapid descent to the river—just at the station a depth of some 80 feet—covered in all directions with luxuriant groves of bananas. Looking from the station up and across the Congo, the prospect presented to the eye is one of no small beauty, the distant hills being of considerable elevation, broken and diversified with cliff and wood. The station buildings comprised one long house facing the Kwa for the accommodation of European officers and travellers—(two were originally built, but with such indifferent skill, that one had gone completely to ruin)—a storehouse, kitchen offices, a row of workmen's huts, and a house for the women of the station. There was also a large boathouse at the landing-place. The station is in no way palisaded or enclosed, except by the beautiful banana plantations with which it is surrounded. Such was the *rendezvous* of our expedition—the point at which, bidding farewell to the milder populations of the Middle Congo districts and to the incipient influences of civilisation, we were to enter upon a region seen only once before by the eye of civilised man—a region whose inhabitants were known for the most part, so far as they were known at all, only as cruel and ferocious savages, as cowardly robbers of the helpless stranger. It may be well, therefore, at this point in our narrative to pause, and give some account of Lieut. Wissmann's experience of those wretches past whose lurking dens we were about to escort the faithful companions of his perilous voyage, as well as of those companions themselves, their country, and their neighbours.

When Lieut. Wissmann was preparing, with Calemba's aid, to embark his expedition upon the Kasaï, he constructed his canoes (in number about thirty), and launched the whaleboat, which he had brought with him overland in sections from Malange, at a point on the Lulua that was believed by him, though erroneously, to be below the last cataract on that river. Passing down to the Kasaï without disaster of any kind, excepting the loss of a canoe, carried over the Lulua Falls above the confluence of the Luebo, and voyaging on as far as the Luangi, it was observed one morning when preparing to leave camp, some of the canoes having already started, that the native women, who had come in early for the purpose of bartering provisions, retired suddenly, and without any apparent cause. This was at once noted as an unfavourable omen, and in re-embarking Lieut. Wissmann and his European subordinates were prepared to defend themselves with their rifles. Scarcely had the canoes pushed off than a flight of arrows from the surrounding jungle fell thickly around them, and the everlasting tomtom of their war-drums, with mingled yells and screams resounding through the forest on all sides, declared plainly enough the hostility of the natives. Happily no one was seriously injured by the arrows, and as standing orders had been issued that on any appearance of danger all the canoes should mass themselves together, the firing, which was renewed again and again, served to congregate the flotilla into a compact body. This was most fortunate, as a much more daring onslaught of the savages was to follow. Immediately from every creek and cranny along the woody shore multitudes of canoes shot out filled with armed men, stalwart warriors standing in each prow, balancing huge spears, in readiness to hurl them whenever the lessening distance should allow their doing so with deadly effect. The way down-stream thus barred, flight became impossible, and resistance inevitable. Accordingly, as quickly as may be, the crack of the elephant-rifle answers the fiendish war-cries of the foe and the whirring of the arrows. One and another of the advancing canoes stop in their progress, and then, sinking or unmanned, drift down the stream; where but a moment before the frenzied robber gloried in the spoil of life and property of which he deemed himself secure, there, when the light rifle-smoke clears off, is seen only a ruddy tinge upon the rippling eddy, a sinking boat, or maybe a dark body drifting with the flood. And thus a way being cleared, the gallant little fleet sail on downstream; but as they go, each bend and turning in the river bank unmasks a new band of robber vessels, and the sickening, hopeless contest has to be renewed. Night—an anxious troubled night it was, a sandy island being the only practicable camping-ground—and night alone, puts a temporary end to this war *à l'outrance*. Nor does the morrow or several succeeding days bring safety or even immunity from molestation. The camps have always to be pitched on islands when the darkness closes on those days of watchfulness and care. One day, towards the end of the long-continued flight, Lieut. Wissmann chanced to turn his head to look upstream. It was well that he did so. Two of the hindmost canoes had most unluckily got into shoal water, and finally had run aground. Their crews were making what haste they could to push them off, when instantly their ever-watchful enemy comes down upon them, and men and helpless women and their infants will certainly be murdered before help can come, or their absence from the company be even noticed. But just in time the whaleboat slackens her pace downstream, and with rapid strokes turns back upon her way. A few sharp shots are fired, and once again the would-be spoilers are themselves despoiled. The stranded boats are rescued, and proceed upon their voyage. At last, after eight days of the keenest anxiety and most wearisome exertion, the expedition entered a less inhospitable region, and glided forth at last upon the longed-for waters of the mighty Congo.

"Congo manena!" ("great is the Congo"), the Bashilangé chief exclaimed whose canoe first gained its stream; and "Congo Manena" he has ever since been called.

With regard to Lieut. Wissmann's Baluba allies, it is to be observed that they form that portion of the nation known as Bashilangé, and are a distinct tribe from the Baluba properly so called, who inhabit a country to the east of the Sankoro, and between the seventh and eighth parallels of south latitude, from which the Bashilangé have migrated at no very remote period to their present domains, which extend westwards from the Sankoro to the Kasaï. The people whom they have probably displaced by thus intruding into the country to the west of their original home are the Bakété, the remnants of which nation, divided into two very unequal portions. now occupy widely separated strips of country, between which the great bulk of the Bashilangé population is to be found. Though much divided into sub-tribes, the Bashilangé are all the subjects of Calemba, whose capital, known as Kashia Calemba, is near the Lulua, and a short distance south of the sixth parallel. It is extremely difficult to estimate their numbers, but they may be roughly set down as about 80,000. In form they are large of stature and very tall, rather dark and coarse-featured, but not stupid or unintellectual in look. Like all negro races with which I am acquainted, they are easily excited to any imaginable degree of frenzy. Their insensibility to pity, their natural cruelty, and their untruthfulness are also characteristics possessed by them in common with other negro tribes. Not so, however, are their virtues, which are in my experience, unhappily, almost unique in Africa. They are thoroughly and unimpeachably honest; somewhat reserved in speech; brave to foolhardiness; and faithful to each other and to their superiors, in whom, especially if Europeans, they place the most complete absolutely unquestioning reliance. They are prejudiced in favour of foreign customs rather than otherwise, and spontaneously copy the usages of civilisation. They are warm-hearted and affectionate towards their friends, and especially their kinsfolk, and they are the only African tribe amongst whom, in their primitive state, I have observed anything like a becoming conjugal affection and regard. To say nothing of such recommendations as their emancipation from fetishism, their ancient abandonment of cannibalism, their heretofore most happy experience of

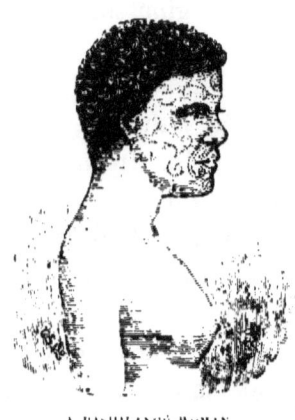

A BASHILANGE WOMAN.

THE BASHILANGE AND THEIR NEIGHBOURS. 21

Europeans, and their national unity under the sway of a really princely prince, I believe them to be the most open to the best influences of civilisation of any African tribe whatsoever. Of their neighbours, by far the most powerful and important are the Bakuba, equal at least to the Bashilangé in numbers, and like them united under a king called Lukwengo; but he is a suzerain of inferior sovereigns rather than the personal ruler of a nation. He is, moreover, himself a fetish institution, and his authority is bound up

A CHIPLUMBA MAN WEARING
MATCHIOKO HEAD-DRESS.

A CHIPLUMBA WOMAN.

with fetishism and is maintained by it. When the present Lukwengo succeeded to the throne, 2000 human victims (slaves) were sacrificed to the *manes* of his predecessor. The Bakuba are a brave and warlike people—thieves and liars, but not cannibals. They are extremely skilful in most native arts. Their cloth, woven in elaborately ingenious and beautiful patterns, would not discredit the manufacturing skill of the most advanced civilised nations, and their work in iron and copper is not less admirable. They are excellent huntsmen and very expert fishermen; but they are not at present open to the influences of civilisation, as Lukwengo has prohibited the introduction of European merchandise into the country, and has confined all intercourse between his people and Europeans within very narrow limits.

Their country conjoins that of the Bashilangé on its northern and north-eastern frontiers, and the Bakuba have thus practically in their hands the command of the Lulua, Kasaï, and Sankoro, the main outlets of the Bashilangé country to the world of commerce and civilisation. A small part of their country, next to the Bashilangé, and edging the banks of the Lulua, is inhabited by the northern and larger section of the Bakètè before referred to, a people who occupy much of our attention in the narrative of our station at Luebo, on which account I shall describe them more fully elsewhere. Another small nation or tribe, residing in a country chiefly surrounded by Bakuba, are the Shammatuka. Their characteristics are Bakuba, but they are subject to their own chief, Bakwengi Babiaha. They are a troublesome people, probably because of their singularly unfortunate relations with Calemba and Lukwengo, two masters whom they pretend to serve, but whom they strive to play off against each other. The Tucongo are a large, powerful, and savage nation, of whom very little is known. Their characteristics are Baluba. Their territory borders upon the Kasaï, and forms a great portion of the western frontier of the Bashilangé, south and south-west of whom are the Bailunda, a wild, savage, and extremely numerous people, united under a chief of large ideas, Matjambo. The Matchioko are a large tribe, residing in a territory between the Tucongo and the Bailunda. They are very ingenious in their manufactures, and as iron-workers are unrivalled amongst the natives, many of the race being constantly resident with the neighbouring tribes in the capacity of blacksmiths. The tribal speciality is, however, their great fondness of trade: they are to be found all over the country swindling their less wily neighbours, and making mischief of all kinds in order to serve their own ends. The Balungu are a large nation whose territory is far to the south, south-east, and east of the Bashilangé. Little was known of them at the time to which my narrative refers, though I have something more to say of them in its place. The other neighbours of the Bashilangé beside the Baluba are two nomadic tribes of dwarfs, the Batua Bankonko and the Batua Basinji, and are probably the dwarfs referred to by Stanley under the name of Wantu. Both tribes are incorrigible thieves, and being nomads, and destitute therefore of plantations, they live habitually by robbing those of the settled tribes. They are excellent warriors, and very hardy and impudent, so that the more otiose and supine of the peoples on whom they prey suffer most. Thus the Bakété are the principal victims of the Batua Bankonko, whose line of march lies in their direction, while their Bakuba neighbours get off almost scot-free. It only remains for me to say a few words as to the general character of the Bashilangé country before returning from this long digression to the thread of my narrative. This territory, measuring about 180 miles from north to south and 160 miles from east to west, lies wholly within the Congo basin, although containing and crossing the watersheds of several rivers. It is abundantly watered, and may be described as undulating land with fine rolling plains, intersected with deep gullies: a grassy country with rich timber on the hillsides and river slopes, except in the basin of the Luebo and a few other isolated districts of luxuriant forest. The soil is exceedingly fertile; but although the country is very thinly inhabited, game cannot be called abundant.

The waters up which our course was to be threaded being at that time unsurveyed and unsounded, it was deemed advisable to lighten both vessels as far as possible before leaving the Congo. The 9th of October therefore found us fully occupied in disembarking whatever we could possibly dispense with, and in procuring such provisions as were requisite for our absolute wants. The next day we left Kwamouth at about 11 A.M., and steamed close along the right bank of the Kwa, here a very crooked river, and were soon out of sight of the Congo. The stream gradually widens, but the scenery continues uninteresting for a very considerable distance. The banks are destitute of forest, and rise gradually and in a somewhat terraced manner into ranges of low hills. Indeed the whole country on both sides of the river may be described as undulating prairie land. By degrees, as we advance up the stream, the country becomes better wooded. Sparsely scattered clumps and single trees, either edging the water or nestling in the hollows between the offshoots of the hills, give variety, and impart a park-like appearance to the landscape. After passing Mulèo, a small village on the right bank inhabited by Bayanzi, we meet with islands where the river broadens considerably. Here we crossed the river, and having passed Ntima on the right bank, recrossed to Mbembo, half a mile above which place we pitched our camp for the night. In the morning we were all afoot early; but owing to the time absorbed in going through the roll-call of so large a body of men, and in reducing them and our heterogeneous living cargo to something like order, discipline, and travelling arrangement, we did not renew our voyage until after 10 A.M. Keeping still to the right bank, we soon became involved in the intricacies of sandbanks and winding channels, alike unexplored and invisible. The Kwa is here lacustrine in character, of immense breadth, and with an almost imperceptible current. At 2 P.M. we stopped at the mouth of a small stream, entering the Kwa from the north. Nothing of importance occurring, we steamed away about 7 A.M., and after considerable trouble amongst the sandbanks, which are here extremely numerous, we stopped at a village on the left bank, the name of which we were unable to discover, as the natives had fled at our approach. This village was partially surrounded by a grove of lofty trees (ironwood or mahogany), which were occupied by a numerous colony of herons. What had induced these usually shy birds to build so near the haunts of man it is impossible to say, but they were discovered to be not the only inhabitants of the grove. On Drs. Wolf and Leslie proceeding to shoot two or three of the herons, the report of their fowling-pieces disturbed a multitude of enormous bats, which continued to flit about in the daylight for some time. Of course we did not occupy the village, which would almost certainly be infested with vermin of many kinds, but an excellent camping-ground near by, a strip of grassy land well raised over the river level. We found an abundance of wood suitable for fuel at this place, which, by-the-bye, is probably situated on an island. Below it a water channel enters the river from the south, and as it discharges the same kind of water, it probably emanates from it higher up. Should such be

WABUMA FISHING-TOWN AND HERONRY.

the case, however, the channel must make a considerable detour, as the island it encloses, if island it be, is manifestly a very large one. It is worthy of note, moreover, that the town is occupied, probably as a fishing-station, only by the Wabuma, whose territory, strangely enough, is supposed to lie wholly on the other side of the river.

Before proceeding, we shipped a quantity of wood, and left about 9 A.M. on the 13th of October. We crossed to the opposite bank, and observed a low range of hills running to the north-east, which showed upon their rain-washed sides large patches of yellow and red laterite: a mass of castellated-looking rock appearing on their summits here and there reminded one not a little of the hills and ruined castles of the Rhineland. Steaming along the right bank, we came shortly to the first of the Musjie villages; distinct clusters of huts, each cluster being inhabited by one combined family, and surrounded by plantations of bananas, manioc, &c. These villages are under the rule of a queen, Gànkabé, whose residential village is in the centre of her curiously separated metropolis, and is distinguished by a higher stockade and larger huts than those erected for the use of her subjects. Here the river Nzali Mpini, which flows from Lake Léopold II., enters the Kwa from the north-east. We parted from our consort for the purpose of more thoroughly exploring this confluent portion of the river; the *Stanley* taking a southern and more direct course up the main stream of the Kwa, while we, going at first in a north-easterly direction and towards Lake Léopold II., passed completely round the larger island lying in the embouchure of the Nzali Mpini, and regained the main channel after pursuing a tortuous course through a maze of sandbanks. The river Kwa here makes a change in the direction of its course, which has been hitherto generally from east to west: from this point the general direction is from south-east to north-west. Here, too, we leave the comparatively known portion of the Kwa, and approaching

Bibòko, on the eastern or right bank, commence what may be more strictly called our voyage of discovery. From Bibòko we crossed between sandbanks and shallows to Kokòro on the left bank, where we spent some time in cutting and shipping a good supply of wood, which is there sufficiently abundant. The natives seemed to be exceedingly wild and impudent, and anything but friendly. As they were crowding round the men and boat, evidently intent upon thievery, it was necessary to disperse them—a feat which we speedily accomplished, and in an amusing manner, by turning on the crowd a steam-pipe. This having the desired effect, we left Kokòro without further adventure, and keeping along the same bank, stopped for the night some two hours later at Mallagohòno. Here we found an abandoned town—deserted probably by its inhabitants in consequence of the death of their chief—surrounded by thick wood, of which we lost no time in obtaining as large a supply as we could load on the boat. This wood-cutting is the main occupation of the crew every evening—and a wearisome duty it is. The cooks are of course exempt, for they have to ply their art simultaneously, but every one else has to fall to with axe or saw, and if we camp at sundown, the task is rarely done before 9 P.M.

It has often occurred to me, when on duty at this weird-looking and vexatious labour, so indispensable to our existence on the river, that it is in some respects an encouraging type, and, as it were, a miniature, of the task we have undertaken for Africa. The deep silence of the woods immediately beside the river—no place is less resonant than the forest—

devours the echo of the axe blow, the rasping of the saw. The firelight irradiates but a few yards of grass and shrubs, and glints on leathery leafage of more distant trees, but only soon to die in the unfathomable depths of outer darkness. Meantime the wood-pile grows, and as the river murmurs by in its eternal ebb, our task is done. Not otherwise the greater life-war that we wage with ignorance and barbarism in Africa, their last great stronghold in the world. Amid the wilderness, how limited the civilising influence of each station! How vain, too, seems the noble holocaust of human life, those lives in which, alas! we are compelled to lay the deep foundations of regenerated social life in Africa! How firm the grasp with which the pioneer must hold the gospel of all human progress and true conquest, even that "whosoever shall seek to save his life shall lose it; and whosoever shall lose his life shall preserve it;" yet surely as the river of our time flows on to the great ocean of eternity, our work is done, the toilsome task achieved.*

This portion of the river is extremely broad, the opposite shore being almost invisible, and the current, at the season at which we ascended the stream, imperceptible. Next morning, proceeding on our voyage, we found the river narrowing, and on rounding the first point we encountered a decidedly rapid current. Intending to keep to the left

---

* Since these remarks were written, I have heard with deep regret of the loss which the Baptist Missionary Society has recently (July 1888) sustained in the deaths of my kind friend Mr. Darling of Lutété, and of Mr. Comber, the head official of the Society's Mission on the Congo. The latter gentleman, universally respected for his high character and kindly disposition, was, I believe, the last of three brothers who have all fallen victims to the climate, and to their devotion to the cause of humanity and religion in this part of Africa.

shore, we had to content ourselves with coasting along and outside an island which was separated from that bank by a narrow and unnavigable channel, from which it is probable that watercourse emanates which I mentioned before as coming out into the main stream again below the deserted Wabuma fishing-village. Still keeping to the same bank, we arrived at Nkûlé, where we crossed to the eastern side of the river. Thence we kept on up-stream a short distance, and recrossing to Nganebecca, where we found the *Stanley* awaiting us, we pitched camp. Next morning, passing through numerous groups of islands—uninteresting in every way—we crossed opposite to two small villages, above which the river narrows to a little over a mile in width. Keeping along the same bank, we were abreast at 2 P.M. of the mouth of the Kwango river, and thus arrived at the termination of that portion of the stream known as the Kwa.

Mount Peigné.

HUT NEAR MOUNT POGGÉ.

CHAPTER III.

Huts at Bosjie—River nomenclature—Forest villages and market-places—Excellent native iron-work—Mount Poggé—Probable embouchure of the Lukenyé—Curious huts—Timidity of the inhabitants—An uncomfortable night—Hippopotami, buffaloes, and cowbirds—Accident to the *Stanley*—Hostility of the Basongo-Meno—Their towns and punishment—A jovial chief—Repairs to the *Stanley*—The expedition nearly blown up—The Luangi—An unknown tribe—A night upon the river.

PROCEEDING a short distance up the Kasaï, we encamped for the night at a village called Bosjie.* Here we noticed that

* There is another Bosjie mentioned by Stanley farther down the river. The Bosjie mentioned in the text I have named for distinction's sake after its discoverer "Bosjie-Massari."

32   UNDER THE LONE STAR.

the form of the huts is distinctly different from that adopted in the lower courses of the Kwa and Congo. They are circu-

HUTS AT BOSJIE-MASSARI.

lar in plan, and in elevation conical, somewhat resembling in outline a North American Indian wigwam, while the inhabitants seemed to be of another, and, it is possible, a mixed race. The riparian scenery, too, of the Kasaï above its junction with the Kwango is, for some distance, very different from that of the united rivers below, being richly wooded not only at the water's edge, but, so far as we could observe, for a great distance inland. In fact, the junction of the Kwango with the Kasaï marks a natural division in the conformation of the drainage system of which it forms a part. The Kwango rises in the high country about Kassange, some 220 miles from the coast, and running north-east. after a sinuous course of about 900 miles, in which it makes a very considerable descent, it pours its waters into the Kasaï in latitude 3.40° south, and longitude 17.10° east. The Kwango is the first large tributary river possessing a really independent existence, source, and system, that enters the Kasaï, or whatever we are to call the great river joining the Congo at Kwamouth. I say "the first," because the Nzali Mpini, whether pouring additional waters into the Congo by its union with the Kwa or merely returning to the main stream the water originally derived from it through Lake Léopold II. or not, is only a short river, lying wholly in the Congo valley, and at an inconsiderable distance from the main stream, to which its course is nearly parallel. The Kwango is not navigable except for a short distance above its mouth, and at certain points higher in its course, and we did not, both on this account, and because we knew that the exploration of the Kwango was occupying the individual attention of more than one explorer, trouble ourselves to make any investigation of its embouchure.*

* Vide Appendix D.

On October 16th we did not continue our journey until near mid-day, when, steaming up-stream, we found the river narrowing to half a mile in breadth, and in some places even less. The channel, too, was much impeded with sunken rocks, which, amid the swiftly rushing waters, made navigation both difficult and dangerous. Leaving these narrows behind us, at 2 P.M. we entered a rapidly spreading sheet of water, where, the current gradually vanishing, we made good progress, and, crossing to the left bank, we passed many small villages, the inhabitants of which crowded their landing-places to witness the unwonted sight which we presented. These villages are built on the very brink of the river, and amid the densest forest, apparently spreading for a considerable distance in all directions; but as there were almost no clearings round the houses, nor signs of any gardens or plantations beyond a few banana trees, it is probable either that the country in their rear is more open than it seems, or that the inhabitants are fishermen who obtain their grain by barter. I incline to think the latter view of the case the correct one, because I observed in the vicinity of several of these villages the largest market-places that I have seen anywhere in the Congo State. At night we encamped on a small open plain raised high over the river level, and above laterite cliffs below which our steamers were moored. At a short distance were two villages, whose inhabitants fled at our approach, but recovering their courage by degrees, found heart, in the morning, to venture into camp with various articles for exchange. Besides provisions, they brought several weapons that displayed their skill as iron-workers—*e.g.*, arrow-heads, spears, knives, &c. When one considers the circumstances under which these people must have to work, and the tools at their command, their success in turning out such excellent specimens of workmanship is almost marvellous. Their iron is, we found, obtained from the ferruginous deposit of certain small streams, which being collected during the dry season, is made into cakes, and stored for use as occasion may demand. In what manner this iron is made ready for the anvil I did not learn, but the tools with which they fashion it are, besides their anvils and bellows, which resemble those used elsewhere on the Congo, pincers of iron, and pounders of hard water-worn stone. Leaving our moorings, we steamed away uneventfully until 3 P.M., when we made fast to a high bank on the same side of the river, where a small native village, excellently placed for defence, was deserted at our approach. This is a good place for wooding, and, as a matter of fact, one of the last before coming to a part of the river's course in which we experienced no small difficulty in obtaining fuel, owing to the remarkable absence of wood on both banks. On the 18th, before we started again on our way, some of the natives came in to see us, amongst them a chief carrying as a sceptre or emblem of office a human thigh-bone, from which circumstance, and from other symptoms of extreme savagery, we concluded that they belonged probably to those cannibal tribes against which the natives lower down-stream had frequently warned us. This morning Mr. Vander Felson was taken ill with fever, and Mr. Olsen accordingly came on board to navigate the *En Avant.* Nothing of any moment occurred this day, during which we kept mainly to the left bank, but on the 19th we encountered numbers of hippopotami, who fled, however, at our approach. The 20th we spent in camp, or, rather, in shooting in its vicinity. Amongst the game secured was an eland and a female hippopotamus, of which the Baluba made a royal feast. On the 21st, about 11 A.M., we sighted Mount Poggé, so called by Lieut. Wissmann after Dr. Poggé, under whose command he had made his *début* as an African explorer. It is a round-topped hill, bare of trees on the summit, and reaching an elevation which cannot greatly exceed 400 feet above the water, but from the abrupt manner in which it rises from the river plain, most noticeable as a landmark. Its lower platform would serve as an excellent site for a station; easily defensible, commanding the adjacent country far and near, and probably the most healthy locality for a very wide distance around. Mount Poggé is the apparently highest and terminating point of a range of low hills running in a north-easterly direction from the river, which assumes again at this point a lacustrine character. It is from 3 to $3\frac{1}{2}$ miles broad, though navigation is much impeded by sandbanks and islands. The latter, mostly large and grassy, are inhabited by fishermen, whose light canoes are constantly to be seen passing in and out of the winding channels and reedy shores. I am myself of opinion that the river Lukenyé enters the Kasaï from the east behind these islands.* The general conformation of the surrounding country shows that a large river must descend from that quarter, and the shape of the Kasaï itself seems to confirm that hypothesis. Time forbade our doing more than making an extremely superficial investigation of the inner channels between the islands, but we found a considerable flow of

* Vide Appendix E.

water setting outwards in all of them. We formed our camp on the left bank of the Kasaï, and therefore opposite Mount Poggé, at 2 P.M. I was sent forthwith by Dr. Wolf in our whaleboat with ten men to visit some villages upon the hillside which we observed from our camp embowered in plantains, the most luxuriant I had seen since leaving the coast. Our errand was to procure provisions, and to ascertain the race and disposition of the inhabitants. Landing, and leaving the boat in charge of two men, I entered the nearer of the two villages, some two hundred yards from the beach. Finding that the inhabitants had fled, probably at the first sign of our approach, I pushed on to the second village, but with no better result. Sending the men to forage as best they might, I took the opportunity of observing the structure of the houses. These were framed with stout timber of various kinds, covered with bamboo on the walls, the roofs being thatched with grass and broad leaves. They were of unusual height for native dwellings, with eaves at least ten feet from the ground, and being rectangular in plan, are gabled with widely projecting roofs. Their great peculiarity, however, consists in the way in which the entrance door is contrived: it might indeed be better called a window. The sill or threshold of this door is about ten feet from the ground, and is gained by mounting upon a staging or platform some five feet in height. Internally there must be a ladder or movable steps, though in those houses into which I looked there was a sheer descent to the floor level. This form of door seems to denote a people constantly at variance with neighbouring tribes, and needing some form of protection against sudden surprises or attempted robbery. I may perhaps as well note that whenever, through the flight of the inhabitants, we were unable to arrange any exchange for the provisions we required, we made it our practice to take what we wanted, leaving instead thereof its full value in merchandise or cowries. During the night we had our first experience since leaving the Pool of really heavy rain. There were only a few peals of thunder, but from soon after sunset until sunrise the rain descended in torrents. I had rather a dismal time of it, as it was my duty to turn out from time to time to see that the sentries were at their posts; otherwise we were fairly comfortable ourselves: our unhappy people were in sorry plight, poor things! The morning was bright and clear, and on leaving our moorings we parted company with the *Stanley*, and proceeded along the right shore, to which we crossed, our consort keeping to the bank on which we had encamped. We met with great difficulty in navigating the shallow and intricate channels, and had as frequently the delay and trouble of pushing the steamer off. However, we circumnavigated a multitude of islands, some little better, indeed, than sandbanks, but the great majority of them wooded more or less, and inhabited seemingly by fishermen, who, a guilty conscience, doubtless, driving them, precipitately fled at our approach, scurrying to the mainland as fast as their canoes could be made to bear them. Hippopotami swarmed in the narrow creeks and channels that we had to thread, and on the mainland bank we once saw a fine herd of buffaloes standing partly in the sedge, a crowd of snow-white cowbirds hopping from back to back. No sooner did they see us, than, with tails erect, they scampered off with many an angry snort across the plain. At about 5.30 P.M. we regained the main channel of the Kasaï, and came up with the *Stanley*, on speaking with whose people we were informed that they had been fired upon by the Basongo Meno* at a town lower down the river, and in return had dispersed their assailants, exacting some little satisfaction in the way of ivory tusks, &c. Landing on a grassy island, where we designed to encamp for the night, it was curious to observe the Baluba dividing themselves into scouting parties for the purpose of searching every tussock of grass and bush that could afford shelter to an enemy. This they did unbidden, but doubtless scenting danger, or perhaps instinctively after the encounter of the day : the first active manifestation of hostility we had met with from the natives in our ascent of the river. This search being completed to the entire satisfaction of our friends, we pitched camp, watch being kept all night by squads of Baluba who volunteered for the service. Shortly after leaving camp next morning, and while we were following in her wake, the *Stanley's* pump broke down, and she had to be moored at once on the nearest island for repairs. We utilised the remainder of the day in helping the *Stanley's* people to re-assort her freight. On the 24th, Dr. Wolf judging that the towns which we should probably pass to-day ought to be punished for their barbarous attack upon Lieut. Wissmann's expedition, we left the *Stanley* still repairing damages, and having taken on board the *En Avant* as large an armed force as she could carry, and taking in tow also the whaleboat.

* Vide Appendix F.

similarly laden, we proceeded to the landing-places of the towns indicated. Leaving the boats in charge of Mr. Olsen. Mr. Vander Felson being still indisposed, we sent on an advanced party of six men under the interpreter Humba, with orders to keep about 200 yards ahead of the main body. At first our path lay through dense jungle, on clearing which, and debouching upon an open space planted with maize, &c., we heard a volley discharged—as it afterwards transpired—by our advanced party against a body of natives who had attacked them. This *rencontre* resulted in the death of one of the attacking party, and the flight of the rest. Proceeding through a plantation, we came to a small village of some fifty huts, similar in structure to those I have described as being near to Mount Poggé. As this place was deserted, we passed on at once to the main portion of the town, which we found to be regularly built, and in a state of thorough order and cleanliness. The paths were all disposed at right angles to each other, and every hut was surrounded with cultivated borders planted with a species of hemp (*Cannabis indica*). The larger plantations and clearings surrounding the town had been recently harvested: there remained only the newly sown maize and ground-nuts beginning to break through the soil. The town being, like its suburb, completely deserted, we had an excellent opportunity of examining the domestic arrangements and economy of the inhabitants. Inside the huts, in addition to the more usual cooking-pots of rude earthenware, spoons of wood or of shell, wooden platters, rough sleeping mats, and the like, we found a large number of ivory pestles, formed of the solid portion of small elephant tusks—an unmistakable sign of the owners' entire isolation from commercial intercourse with the outer world. Of arms, we obtained a great quantity of arrows, some tipped with iron, a few with copper, but by far the greater number made from the central spine of the palm-leaf, the points being encrusted with poison; also a number of bows, which we destroyed before leaving, when we appropriated all that was worth removing. Proceeding to examine a house, we found a considerable difference as to length between the interior and exterior measurements. As this could only be accounted for by assuming that there was some narrow compartment formed in the width of the end wall opposite to the entrance door or window, or, more correctly, between the outer wall and a false one within, we essayed to make trial of this theory, and were rewarded by discovering in every house a secret store, which, being filled with provisions of all kinds, yielded both an immediate supply for our wants, and a satisfactory solatium for the wrongs of Lieut. Wissmann's party. All the houses consisted of one apartment, except that which we supposed belonged to the chief, and which, although not so very much larger than those of his subjects, was subdivided into three, but there was no store or concealed compartment at the end. Externally this house was distinguished by an enclosure of palm fronds, by its greater height, and by many trophies of the chase. Having collected as much agricultural produce and stores as the men could carry, as well as the more valuable of the household utensils and arms, and capturing as much live stock as came in our way, we retraced our steps to the steamer after setting fire to the houses. On passing the spot where the native party had met our advance, and where the body of the man who had been shot lay, we found that a poor little boy had ventured out of the jungle and was weeping beside the corpse, possibly that of his father. We could make nothing of his language, none of our Baluba even being able to interpret his words or to make themselves understood. I proposed to take him with us, that, after a civilising process, we might return him some day to his people, and by him explain to them effectually that our disposition was not hostile, save only to the evil-doers of robbery and wrong. Dr. Wolf, however, concluded to leave him, though, fearing the excessive zeal of our savage followers, I waited beside the child until all had passed by. We found Mr. Olsen and the steamer in safety, and duly embarked our booty, wherewith we at once descended the river towards the spot at which the *Stanley* was repairing. On the way down, we stopped at a village which we had passed in the morning, believing it to have been deserted. Approaching the shore, we observed a solitary figure dancing and gesticulating in a violent and eccentric manner. It turned out that this individual was the chief, who, having fortified himself with palm-wine, had thus gained courage to welcome us to his dominions. Unfortunately we could only communicate with him by signs, by which, however, we succeeded in making him understand that we did not intend to do him any injury. Upon this he called loudly to some people concealed in the woods, whence, in response to his cries, several women, and one intelligent and presentable young man, shortly after made their appearance. The women were, indeed, deplorably degraded specimens of humanity, an opinion which

Dr. Wolf's careful examination confirms; the low animal look and expression of their faces being unredeemed by any indication of intellectual force. Their clothing was of the scantiest that I have ever seen; merely a small oblong strip (about three inches by two) of grass-cloth worn in front, a bunch of feathers being deemed sufficient adornment for the back, which articles were connected and maintained in position by a zone of antelope hide. Their teeth were very curiously filed and their bodies gashed with large cicatrices, but we did not observe any tattoo marks. Before we left, our inebriate old friend presented us with two goats and a few bunches of plantains, so, what with one thing and another, when we once more arrived at the *Stanley* we had no difficulty in making ourselves sufficiently welcome by an equitable division of our riches. The people whose towns we had burned, as well as the old chief whom we had afterwards visited, belonged undoubtedly to those tribes known to us as Basongo Meno, a race which I incline to identify with the Tucongo, whose proper territory, however, lies more to the south and south-east.

BASONGO MENO WOMAN.

We spent the 25th of October in camp, as the *Stanley* was still unable to proceed, but her repairs being completed early in the morning of the 26th, we got under way about 8 A.M., and proceeded together up the stream. We stopped at a small village for the purpose of wooding, some miles above the scene of our recent expedition. As usual, the inhabitants had fled at our approach, but we were able the better to examine their town. Here we observed a form of blacksmith's bellows different from any we had seen before: it had four wind-tubes in place of the two generally to be found. In order to deter these people from repeating the sort of conduct they had pursued towards Lieut. Wissmann's expedition, we appropriated the two best canoes we could find, and destroyed the rest. During the afternoon, in ascending the river, we visited four other towns, and destroyed the canoes there also, encamping at night on the right bank. It is to be noted that the stream had again narrowed, the current becoming correspondingly rapid: the banks, also, were again densely wooded. On the 27th of October nothing of any moment occurred, but we observed throughout the day a growing change in the scenery along the river-banks. Wherever the ground was not covered with luxuriant natural forest there were large tracts of land under the richest cultivation,

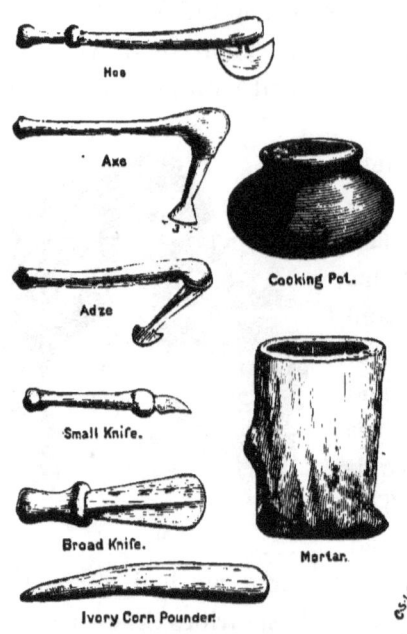

BASONGO MENO IMPLEMENTS.

and the towns built upon the steeply rising shores presented a picturesque and pleasing appearance, being often backed by swelling hills covered with gardens and plantations. In the evening we encamped on the left bank near some villages, the inhabitants of which (still Basongo Meno) came to visit us. They were lighter in colour than those of the same race whom we had seen farther down the river, and were undoubtedly less savage, and more friendly, although so far predatory in their inclinations that a strict watch had to be kept over their movements, in spite of which, however, they contrived to purloin a cartridge-bag, and a few other small articles. They were willing, indeed anxious, to trade, and brought into camp an abundance of fowls, fine fish, bananas, yams, &c., pine-apples, and some excellent palm-wine, of which Mr. Schneider's servant Manoel, who happened to be waiting upon me, imbibed so freely, that he was very near blowing the whole expedition to atoms by brandishing a candle in the neighbourhood of the expense ammunition, which had been placed for security in my tent. Luckily he was caught in time, and promptly punished. At this camp was a magnificent borassus palm, the last we saw in ascending the river.

On the 28th of October we arrived off the mouth of the Luangi. I had remained on board the *Stanley* this day for a little change—Mr. Vander Felson having completely recovered his health and resumed his duties. We encamped for the night on a sand-spit at the confluence, but the *En Avant* did not come up to camp until long after dark. The following day (October 29th) we devoted entirely to exploring the rivers and district generally. It was found that the Luangi was not only choked with sandbanks, and blockaded at its mouth with a bar, but was deficient in flow of water—a remarkable circumstance, considering the length of the river, which must exceed 500 miles. Such water as there was appeared to be much discoloured with laterite. The land to the south-east of the embouchure lies very low, and is, in fact, a swamp covered with dense jungle, extending apparently for a considerable distance inland. On the other side of the Luangi the ground rises into low hills, but is also thickly wooded, and on neither shore did we observe any sign of human habitations or inhabitants. The opposite bank of the Kasaï, however, is well populated, and there are several towns, from which the people crossed to our camp, bringing a variety of articles for barter, including ivory, for which they were desirous of obtaining cop-

BASONGO MENO YOUTH.

per. It is probable that the greater friendliness of these people arises from trade intercourse with Angola. We did not go into the towns, which are palisaded, as if for defence and protection against troublesome neighbours, but, from what we could see of them, we believed the huts to be constructed similarly to those of the Basongo Meno already described. The people themselves we could not identify with any known tribe, but though most like the Basongo Meno, they were evidently much less savage. Although without marks of tattooing, they were curiously gashed both on face and body, the cicatrices presenting often a hideous appearance. Their teeth were not filed, but the two centre teeth in the upper jaw were removed.

Next morning (October 30th), the *Stanley* left the camping-ground, where we had thus passed two successive nights, about an hour and a half before the *En Avant*, to which I had now returned. Consequently it behoved us to hasten as much as possible in overtaking our consort, whereby we once more proved the truth of the old adage, "the more haste the less speed;" for starting without a sufficient stock of firewood, we had to stop at the first place which seemed to promise a supply. This was a spot on the right and inhabited bank of the river, but the natives watched our proceedings in no unfriendly spirit, and we went on our way without further noteworthy incident.

Still endeavouring to overtake the *Stanley*, we steamed on late into the evening instead of mooring the vessel and camping out. We were aware that there were many sandbanks ahead of us in that part of the river in which we had arrived, but hoped that with due care we should avoid them. Unhappily, however, in the gloom we grounded, and though we soon got off again, yet, finding it impossible to free ourselves from the intricacies of the navigation, we were obliged to cast anchor where we were, mid-stream, and spend the night upon the water. We were lying about half a mile from the shore, and through the warm haze of evening the light breeze bore towards us the sound of tom-toms beating in the distant villages, either as a signal of danger, or for the dances with which the natives while away their leisure time. Below, the almost silent river flowed sullenly on to its far-off death in the far-off sea, its soft and soothing music varied only, as the night-advanced, by calls of wandering birds, or broken by the low breathing of

BASONGO MENO MARKET-WOMEN.

the hippopotamus. Lights from the villages glimmered for a time, but died away as the crescent moon rose in the sky, and with swift growing radiance one by one the bright stars shone upon the flood, and tipped its every wavelet with a crest of gold. It seemed to me a solemn hour. The river spoke of fleeting life and sorrowful, lighted but fitfully by worldly hopes and aims; but when these die, as die in time they must, the clear stars told of heavenly visions, bright promises and hopes of a new life-undying, shining ever more and more upon the restless waves of our poor earthly life-stream, on through its night-hours till the sun breaks out and shadow-time is past.

The following morning (October 31st) we got away early, and at last happily made our escape from the difficult position into which we had calmly run ourselves in the dark, but our wood was used up almost to the last log. Luckily we had not far to go before reaching an old plantation on the right bank, where we obtained a small supply of dry wood. A number of women who were working there came down, inspired by friendly curiosity, to look at us. We crossed over to the opposite shore, but meeting with an increasingly strong current, and our wood again threatening to become exhausted, we recrossed the stream to a point at which we saw some market-people making signals to us. From these friendly folk we procured a quantity of excellent fish, and some good palm-wine, and as there was an abundance of wood at hand, we did not neglect to lay in an ample supply. Having fortunately encountered no sandbanks or other obstacles to-day, we sighted the *Stanley* about 4 P.M., moored beside a large island opposite to the mouth of the Sankoro. Rejoining there the main body of the expedition, we found that the natives had already come forward in a friendly manner with provisions, &c., and that it was decided we should remain here for possibly a day.

SHAMMATUKA FISHING-HUTS

CHAPTER IV.

The Sankoro—River nomenclature again discussed—The relative magnitude of the Sankoro and the Kasaï—A picnic—Aquatic birds—Bakuba country reached—A theft and quarrel—The *En Avant* constantly aground—Price of provisions—Friendly natives—The Lulua described—Its fish and fishermen—The end of our voyage.

THE Sankoro at its junction with the Kasaï is considerably the narrower river, but manifestly the weightier body of water, and although its course at this point, and for some distance above it, is south-westerly, and nearly at right angles to that of the Kasaï, which maintains the same direction in its course above the confluence which the united waters possessed below it, I am of opinion that those united waters should be known by the name of the Sankoro,

FISHERMEN OF THE LULUA.

at least as far as the confluence of the Kwango, if not to Kwamouth. My contention briefly is, that while it is *probable* that the Sankoro with its affluents drains as large an area as the Kasaï, and possesses a greater volume of water, it has been *proved* to be navigable for a considerably greater distance, and consequently that it occupies, for the greater distance, the lowest level of the drainage area common to the two rivers and their tributaries. The approximate length of the Sankoro above the confluence is 660 miles, of which more than 300 are navigable. Its general course is first from south to north, thence east to west, and thereafter north-east to south-west. The tributaries on the left bank are the Lubi and the Lubudi, with the Muansangoma, together with several smaller streams. On the opposite bank the chief affluents are the Lomami with its tributary the Lukash. On the other hand, the Kasaï itself, and its only large affluent from the right, the Lulua, have each a length of about 750 miles: the Luebo, one of the largest tributaries of the Lulua, probably exceeds 400 miles in length, but the length of its other tributaries, the Lombali and Miaw, has not been ascertained. The tributaries of the Kasaï on its left bank are, besides smaller streams, the Chipaka and the Chikumba. The Kasaï is navigable for about 100 miles above the confluence with the Sankoro, the Lulua being navigable for about 30 miles above its junction with the Kasaï. The other tributaries are useless practically for purposes of navigation. Undoubtedly the Kasaï was the first discovered and the first explored, and indeed the Portuguese have had a certain cognisance of its existence possibly for centuries; but I must maintain that since physically it is a tributary of the Sankoro, its name ought not to supplant that of the nobler stream whose waters it helps to swell: their confluence is at 4.12° south and 20.25° east.

On the 1st of November, Dr. Wolf, Lieut. Andersson, and myself, with a crew of Zanzibaris, set off in the whale-boat soon after 7 A.M. to explore the embouchure of the Sankoro. We took with us our rifles, provisions for the day, and some instruments. Rowing away from the Kasaï, and up the stream of the Sankoro, we threaded the narrow channel which separates a long and richly-wooded island from the right or north-western bank. This island did not appear to be inhabited, but the splendid growth of timber upon it, and the variety of the trees, embracing the cotton-wood, the mahogany, and the gorgeous crimson-leaved traveller's tree, with its silvery bark, was really remarkable. The neighbouring shore of the mainland was also very thickly wooded, but amongst the forest were several clearings with plantations and villages, the inhabitants of which were friendly, and willing to trade. They sold us some fish of the usual kinds, and a few curios, such as knives and arrows. We purchased from them also a chief's cap of fine workmanship. Coming round the end of the island, which we judged to be about seven miles in length, we regained the main stream through a channel facing some high cliffs of red laterite on the north-western shore, at this point hilly, but a brief space above, and for many miles, low and swampy. We ate our luncheon in the boat, and thereafter proceeded leisurely to descend the river to our encampment at the confluence, where we arrived about 5.50 P.M.

On this day's excursion we observed for the first time in our ascent of these rivers some hippopotamus traps, which, if not unique in plan, are certainly unlike any I have seen lower down the Congo, or elsewhere on the west coast. We secured no game, nor indeed did we see any, except some hippopotami and aquatic birds, of which there was great abundance of all those kinds usually found on the Congo — both grey and large brown herons, pelicans, marabout-storks, adjutants, ibis (black and bronze), flamingoes, snipe, green sandpipers, Egyptian geese, small black and white teal, black darters, waterhens, and the common wild duck of the African west coast. These last are about the same size as the European mallard, but utterly unlike in plumage: the head is chocolate-coloured with black neck-ring, the back and wing-covers grey, the breast and under part of body silver-grey, the legs and feet black, the bill also black, with yellow mandible. Just before reaching our camp we witnessed a glorious sunset. The sun went down behind the wooded hills and lofty red cliffs on the other side of the Kasaï, casting for a short time a deep shadow on the farthest portion of the river spreading out

HIPPOPOTAMUS TRAP.

before us. From behind the darkened hills the light streamed up with intense brilliance, illumining as against an opalescent sky a multitude of cloudlets, dyeing them with the most gorgeous hues of orange and scarlet that could be imagined. But the glory was soon past, and by the time we regained our camp the cool greys and neutral tints of evening were already deepening round us into night. Leaving our camp next morning about 7.50 A.M., we proceeded up the stream of the Kasaï, passing many wooded islands and sandbanks. We came up with the *Stanley* moored at an island close to the right bank, which is, at this point, richly clothed with forest, and diversified with hills and cliffs. The opposite shore is a complete contrast, being very low and swampy, and that for a considerable distance. Here we encamped and set our people early to their nightly task of cutting wood, of which there was an abundance.

BAKUBA HEAD-DRESS.

The natives, who are Bakuba, we found friendly, and for the first time in our ascent of the river we saw the distinctive Bakuba head-dress—a small cap of fine grass, beautifully woven, and worn on the extreme back of the head, where it is fastened by pins of iron or copper. The sight of this national badge greatly rejoiced the hearts of our Baluba, who had been secretly fearing that they would never see their native country again. We noticed that these people had bows and arrows precisely similar to some that we had purchased at the Sankoro.

On the 3rd of November we were early informed that one hold of the *Stanley's* had been broken open, and that a load of salt, and the same weight of cowries, had been abstracted. This theft had been committed during the night, and such an air of mystery pervaded the whole occurrence, that we were quite unable to discover the thieves. We suspected some of our Zanzibaris, but could not prove our suspicions. Leaving camp and proceeding up the river, now flowing from S.S.E., we encountered a very much stronger current, the channel having greatly diminished in width and being unobstructed with islands. Steaming on until 2 P.M., we moored on the right bank, where we found a good wooding-place. Here one of our Baluba picked a quarrel with a Bakuba who had come to our people offering palm-wine for sale. Our man seized upon the wine, and refused to pay anything for it. As he was distinctly in the wrong and very violent, we vindicated justice by punishing him severely. I had spent the whole day on board the *Stanley*, finding it a pleasant change, as, having no responsibility, I had more leisure to observe the river and riparian scenery. The mean breadth of the stream is, hereabouts, little short of a mile, and both banks are densely wooded.

On the 4th of November we left in the *En Avant* at 7.40 A.M., and after steaming for a short time, again ran upon a sandbank. I say "again" advisedly, for although I have not noted the frequency of such disasters—they were unspeakably vexatious, and trying in every way to one's temper—yet I may as well remark once for all that we were constantly aground. Truly, either the ship or her skipper had a genuine affection for dry land, and it was the more annoying to us, because, although the *Stanley* was a larger vessel, and more heavily laden, she almost never grounded. After half an hour's delay we succeeded in getting off the sandbank, and continued our course between numerous sand-islets on which the fishermen had erected temporary villages and huts, which, with their parti-coloured nets stretched out to dry, the groups of idlers startled into sudden and surprised activity by our approach, whilst others in their boats pursued their calling, presented altogether an animated and ever-changing picture.

On the river-banks were large manioc and banana plantations, and the whole district through which we were now passing appeared to be well cultivated: at any rate, it is a land of plenty, for we found we could purchase two fine capons for one brass rod (value one penny halfpenny), and an excellent goat for two yards of cotton cloth (value fourpence). Coming up at 6.35 P.M. to camp, whither the *Stanley* had preceded us, we learnt that she had been struck by a hippopotamus; she was very slightly damaged, but it is probable that the hippopotamus had more serious occasion to regret the encounter. Starting at 7 A.M. on the 5th, we followed up-stream in the wake of the *Stanley;* but having been unable to obtain any wood at last night's camping-ground, we were soon obliged to stop for fuel at a native landing-place. We had scarcely reached the shore when a crowd of friendly natives gathered to-

The first rapids on the Sulua.

gether, anxious to traffic in any available merchandise, including the always welcome palm-wine, which is, in this part of the continent, almost always used when fresh and non-intoxicating, although it cannot be indulged in with perfect freedom, or beyond the bounds of strict moderation, as it has a tendency to impair the digestive organs, and to injure the health generally. Old palm-wine, and thoroughly fermented, is, in my opinion, an abomination, and it is a powerful intoxicant. It is in its fermented condition that it is generally used farther down the Congo.* Before we resumed our journey, Bakwengi Babiaha, the head chief of the Shammatuka, came to see us. He was extremely well dressed, according to their ideas, and was evidently much respected by the people generally, who grovelled to him in a very abject manner. After exchanging a few presents, and expressing our mutual gratification at meeting, we continued our course about 1.30 P.M., having secured a sufficient supply of wood. Keeping along the right bank, and passing several islands, we sighted the *Stanley* at 5.50, just as she was entering the Lulua. Encountering a strong current, however, and darkness coming on, it was fully 8 P.M. before we gained our camping-ground, being guided to the spot by the fires which the *Stanley's* people had lighted. We found them encamped on a small island in the Lulua, where,

---

* Palm-wine is merely the sap of the palm-tree, and is extracted from several species, notably those known by the natives as Monma (Borassus), Matombé, and Samba. It is obtained by inserting a hollow reed into the stem of the tree immediately below the place from which a frond has been removed. The reed piercing the outer bark, taps the pithy centre of the stem, and so affords ready vent to the rising sap, which exudes through the reed, and is received in a gourd or earthen vessel attached thereto. In process of time this practice slowly kills the tree.

greatly to my comfort, my tent had been already pitched, it, together with my servant, being now generally sent ahead in the *Stanley*. We had some heavy rain during the night, a circumstance that occasioned no small disturbance, for one of the Baluba chiefs—none other than Congo Manena, by-the-bye—being anxious lest some of his goods should be injured by the wet, invaded my tent with them, and gave me no peace until he had piled up a quantity of boxes and things where there was at best but little room.

It was thus that we entered the Lulua, the last stage of our voyage, prevented by the darkness from discerning the landscape, or even observing the nearer features of the riverbanks. The knowledge that we subsequently acquired may as well be given here, since it will thus serve best to complement the following narrative of events. At its embouchure, and for a very considerable distance above the confluence of the Luebo, the Lulua has a mean breadth of 400 yards, and flows between forest-covered hills in a deep though by no means sinuous channel, somewhat impeded in places by rocks and shifting banks of coarse sand. The current is strong, averaging four knots an hour: the water clear, and when placed in a glass, the colour of weak tea. In the rainy season, however, when the level of the river is some ten feet higher than at other times, the water is much discoloured with laterite and the rich red soil through which some of its tributaries, notably the Musisi, drive their course. The navigation of the Lulua ceases at the first rapids, 34 miles above its mouth, but throughout its whole length there are intervals of navigable water. The surrounding

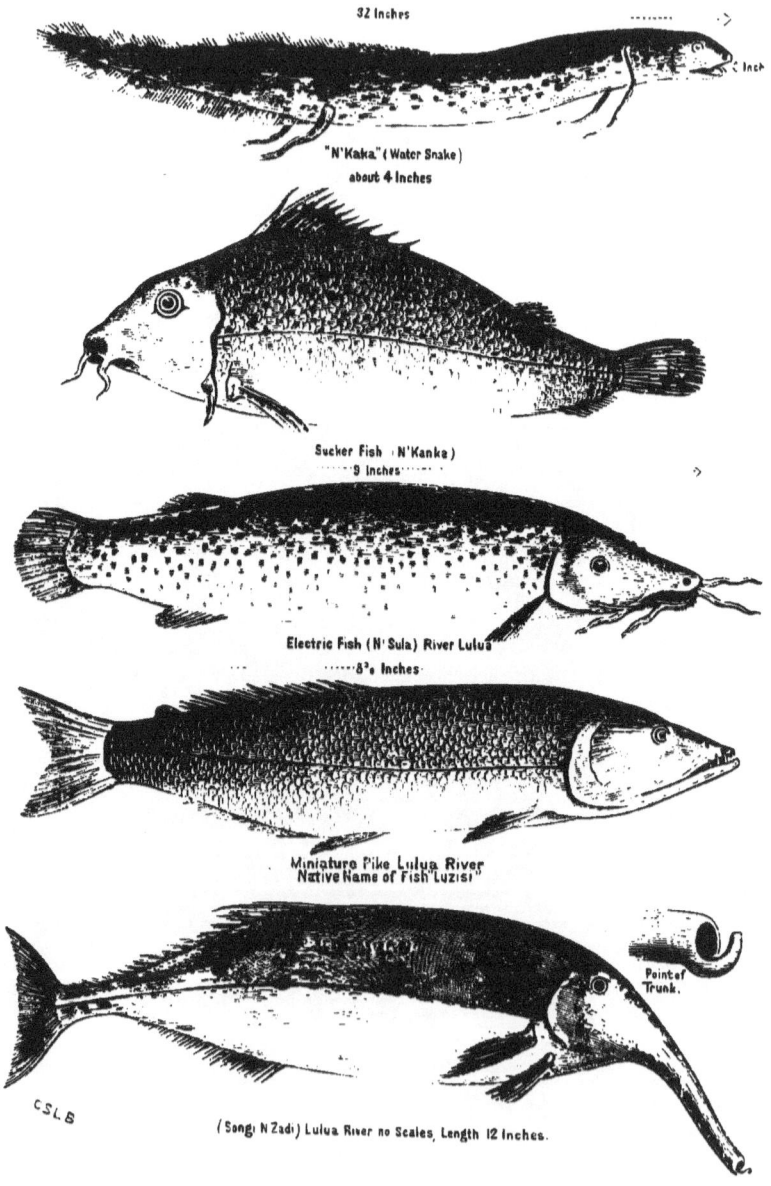

LULUA FISH.

country is all more or less hilly: in the upper part of the river's course bare and treeless, but as the Kasaï is approached, covered with forest, and in some spots with dense jungle. The waters are infested with alligators and crocodiles, enormous dark brown water-rats as large as rabbits, also otters, so that it might well be supposed that, amid such a multitude of enemies, to say nothing of the ravages of all manner of waders and aquatic birds, the fish can have but a precarious existence. They are, however, extremely numerous, and afford occupation and support to a large body of Bakuba and Chiplumba-Baluba fishermen. I observed only three fish (if fish they all can be called) peculiar to the Lulua: one an electric fish, resembling in appearance and habits the well-known catfish; another, a curious creature, destitute of a mouth, but with a long snout terminating in a kind of sucker, with which the natives fancy it lives upon the juices of other fish—they call it Songo Nzadi, i.e., "elephant of the river;" the last is a water-snake about a yard in length, and, so far as I could ascertain, an eel in most of its habits, but with scales and fangs like a genuine serpent. The natives, who will all eat it, call it "Nkaka."

On the 6th we were delayed until 8 A.M. in consequence of our having to take back from our Baluba the arms and ammunition with which we had provided them while in our service, as they were now on the edge of their own territory. This morning, for about an hour, the *En Avant* actually went ahead of the *Stanley*. At 11 A.M. we stopped on the right bank to obtain wood, leaving again about 1.30 P.M., the *Stanley* having passed us in the meantime. At 6.15 P.M. we overtook our consort at a deserted

Shammatuka fishing-village on the same bank, and there encamped. The houses here were totally different from any I had seen farther down the rivers. They are formed entirely with thin stems and leaves of the creeping bamboo, and are of the simplest possible construction. During the day we had seen very few of the natives: they had probably

THE LULUA RAPIDS FROM THE STATION.

gone off in dread of the strangers. There was an appearance of poverty about their belongings quite unaccountable in a country which looked, at any rate, as if well supplied with natural wealth, although the clearings and plantations amidst the luxuriant forest were small and far between. One part of the river passed to-day was narrow, and dangerous with sunken rocks, and the current was very swift.

Leaving early on the 7th, we proceeded up the river, here very rapid, and impeded with dangerous rocks, and arrived about mid-day at our destination, the point at which the river Luebo, coming from the south, falls into the Lulua, which there turns somewhat abruptly in an easterly direction, and where, within half a mile, its navigation is stopped by boiling rapids. We moored our steamer beside the dense bush, where, I could not help recollecting, disconsolately, that my future lot was for a while to be cast, and then began to disembark the Baluba, whose joy at reaching their own territory again was very demonstrative. They had been singing and shouting through the greater part of the past night, and now, when they were put on shore, there was endless capering about, hand-shaking, and the like. They had a long journey before them still, for the distance of Kashia-Calemba from the Luebo is about 122 miles by the native road; but Calemba refused to allow his people to leave us, generously insisting that they should first clear the site of our future station of the primeval forest and jungle. In the meantime he sent messengers on to his capital to announce his return, and to require presents and supplies to be brought to us. Our voyage was now at an end, and when the *Stanley* should begin her descent of the river, those of us who were to be left at Luebo or to go on to Luluaburg * would enter upon a new era in their experiences of life in Africa. In the afternoon we were visited by our neighbours of the Bakètè tribe, whose towns, called Kassengè, were

---

* The station which Lieut. Wissmann had established on the Lulua, near the Bashilangé-Baluba capital, Kashia-Calemba, and where he had left Mr. Bugslag in charge.—Vide *Argument*.

quite near to us, a short distance inland from the right bank of the Lulua. They were very friendly, so that—as all our party were in good health and spirits—our new station was beginning its existence under propitious auspices.

ON THE ROAD TO KASSÈNGÉ

IN KASSÈNGÉ VILLAGE.

CHAPTER V.

Luebo—Its environs and our neighbours—The station site—Departure of the *Stanley*—The log-house—Calemba leaves for Kashïa-Calemba followed by Dr. Wolf—Clearing, levelling, and building—Kassèngé and its plantations—Habits and customs of the Bakòté—Their preparations of tobacco and cassava—Christmas festivities—Daily routine in station—My hospitalities—Sunday in Central Africa—Return of Dr. Wolf for the New Year—His departure in *En Avant* for further exploration of Sankoro—Tragic death of native girl.

THE territory in which we had now arrived formed that part of the Bashilangé country inhabited by the Chiplamba tribe which lies between the Lulua and Kasaï, and terminates towards the north in an apex at the junction of those rivers, which form respectively its eastern and western boundaries: the forests and jungles of the Luebo may be taken as its southern limit. Thus, as it was determined to establish the new station exactly at the mouth of the Luebo valley, we were to be therefore at the extreme verge of the Bashilangé territory, and, so far as intercourse with the native races is concerned, were more likely to come into contact with the Bakété and Bakuba than with the Baluba, the people who had been the means of our coming into the country; for besides a number of Bakuba fishing-towns on the river, by far our nearest and most numerous neighbours were the Bakété, inhabiting Kassèngé, and the villages beyond. The Chiplumba towns nearest to the new station were Beni-Kashia, about twenty-two miles to the southward, and on the road to Luluaburg and Kashia-Calemba; and Biombé, some eight miles to the west, and between the Lulua and Kasaï. Our next neighbours beyond and on the opposite side of the Chiplumba country were the Shammatuka, of whom I have already spoken, and of them, as indeed, I am sorry to say, of the Chiplumba towns also, the remark must be made, that I am glad they were no nearer. In an amphitheatre enclosed by dense forest, the tongue of land which, after some little hesitation, we selected as the actual site of our buildings was of triangular form, being bounded on the north-east by the Lulua, on the north-west by the Luebo, and on the south by the forest and a swampy lagoon, which, by-the-bye, emitted swarms of mosquitos.* The two longer sides of the triangle measured about 200 yards, and the base 150 yards. My own opinion, which subsequent experience and discovery confirmed, was that a far better site could have been found on the opposite side of the Luebo, but the strategic advan-

* Vide Appendix G.

TEMPORARY ARRANGEMENTS.

tages of the position chosen are no doubt great, and of almost primary importance. Of course the first things to be done were to clear at least a portion of the site, and to secure our stores, which had in the first instance to be kept under canvas. We immediately fell to work clearing a site for the tents, but when, after landing such goods belonging to us as she had been laden with, the *Stanley* left us on her homeward voyage, no great progress had been made. Mr. Walker returning with the *Stanley*, Mr. Schneider, armourer to the expedition, remained with us, he having acquired sufficient knowledge of engineering to supply his place. Mr. Vander Felson of course had to stay with his ship, and Dr. Wolf was in command.

THE LOG-HOUSE.

After the clearing, our first and most tedious work was the building of a log-house, doubtless the first of the description, as I hope and believe it will be the last, erected in

Central Africa. It was built on the recommendation of Dr. Leslie, as a ready way of storing our goods until a permanent storehouse should be erected; and as, first and last, it occasioned no small waste of time and labour, and was, moreover, in every respect a failure, I propose giving a few details of its history as a warning to others. Of course we had no plan of the building: it was, as are the great majority of European buildings in the Congo territory, built "out of our heads," as we worked away, while, as none of us had any idea of the principles of construction upon which log-houses are framed, we encountered infinite trouble in fitting the logs to each other, trouble that was crowned by the collapse, or rather bursting asunder, of the edifice when it reached the height of the eaves. We had to begin afresh, and by means of securing the corner upright posts firmly to each other before filling in the walls with logs, we contrived to get the unsightly Canadian nuisance roofed in at last. In size it might have measured about 35 feet by 18 feet, with a height of 12 feet in front and 9 feet behind. Into this building we removed our stores, arms, &c., on the 23rd of November, and hoped that they were safe from the weather as well as from thieves. The first rainstorm undeceived us: the roof being too flat, admitted the water in streams. Dr. Wolf blamed the workmanship—I the design. We agreed that something must be done. Accordingly we covered the roof to a depth of some two inches with puddled clay, and in addition erected an outer roof of leaves and grass to serve as a kind of umbrella. But through the water came, bringing the clay with it, so that now we were in worse case than before. At last, after renewed efforts, we rendered it somewhat less pervious to the weather; and though snakes, scorpions, and other vermin took to it kindly, we contrived to keep our stores in the log-house until, the permanent magazine being completed, we were enabled to demolish it.

In the meantime I had levelled the site and erected the main posts of the storehouse, and our Baluba had built two temporary huts—one for Mr. Schneider, and the other for myself. Dr. Wolf occupied his tent, and Mr. Vander Felson the cabin of the *En Avant*. By this time, too, Calemba and the greater part of his people had gone home. He had stayed with us until after the return of his messengers, which occurred some ten days after the departure of the *Stanley*, and who brought with them a number of goats for a present, as well as Dr. Wolf's saddle-oxen. On leaving, Calemba had bidden Congo Manena and a number of his people to remain for our present assistance. We found them extremely useful, but they were now to depart also, and it was arranged that they should accompany Dr. Wolf on his journey to Luluaburg. After they had all gone, I devoted my attention to the completion of the storehouse and of the clearings, and I began to drain and fence in the station.

While these works were in progress, I often left them in charge of Messrs. Schneider and Vander Felson while I made excursions into the Bakété country * for purposes of policy and exploration. Sometimes, too, I had to cross the Lulua in order to superintend our men when cutting grass for thatching, as we had no grass suitable and near to us

---

* The southern and lesser Bakété country is situated to the south-south-east of the Bashilangé, and is tributary to Matjambo. I never visited it, but I understand it is about 200 miles distant from the Bakété towns near Luebo station.

on our side of the river. Thus I came to make thorough acquaintance with the Bakètè, their customs, state, and language. Physically they are very inferior to the Baluba, though the features of both men and women are more regular and refined than those of any other negro tribe I have ever seen.

The men are somewhat effeminate. Of course they will not work—the African naturally expects the women to do that; but what is unusual, they will hunt and trap only small game, and will not fish at all. Their political condition is significant of their character, for they are tributary to the Bakuba, with the view of obtaining protection against the Batua nomads, who are a trouble to them, chiefly from their own supineness. They are, however, or at least the women are, excellent agriculturists, and their plantations are really most beautiful. The gardens or fields in the immediate vicinity of Kassèngè were altogether so delightful, and surprised me so greatly when I first saw them, brilliant with the yellow blossoms of the pea or ground-nut, and adorned with a multitude of tropical esculents, that I often alluded to the place as the "Garden of Eden." In their seasons I observed manioc, maize, yams, sweet potatoes, sorghum, gourds, okras, beans, peas (resembling the description I have seen of the "mummy

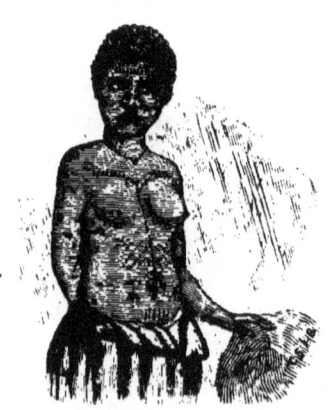

A BAKÈTÈ GIRL.

pea" of Egypt); * also an inferior kind of cabbage, and some plants—(one especially with lovely crimson blossoms)—whose leaves are eaten much as spinach; also pine-apples, water-melons, mangangas (a kind of yellow plum), bananas, plantains, and the species of banyan called "saffu." But what surprised and pleased me was not so much the variety of plants as their cultivation: they were as well grown as they could be, arranged in symmetrical plots and beds, and separated by wide, perfectly straight alleys, weeded, swept, and maintained in the greatest neatness and order. They grow no rice, although their neighbours the Baluba raise large quantities of it.

A BAKÉTÉ MAN.

They cultivate tobacco of an extremely inferior kind,

* My attention has been drawn to an article on the "mummy pea" of Egypt, written by an Irish clergyman, and published some years ago in a popular magazine. It would appear that a few peas found in a mummy case in one of the more ancient Egyptian sepulchres had been sown by some horticulturists, and had, despite their long imprisonment, germinated. The plants proved arborescent in habit, and bore crimson and white blossoms with well-filled pods: the peas when cooked being pronounced excellent. From the entire dissimilarity of these plants (or shrubs, they might be called) from anything of the kind now to be found in Egypt, the writer of the article in question drew some inferences which we may well set aside; he seems to have forgotten that his mummy peas might possibly be identical with species still to be found throughout the interior of Equatorial Africa—as undoubtedly they are. Their presence in the ancient mummy case in Egypt therefore argues, to my mind, an intercourse in the remotest ages between that country and Central Africa through the upper valley of the Nile—an intercourse forgotten now for an immense period, but of which at least one monument still remains in the existence of those vast artificial caves in Kavirondo reported first by Commander Cameron, with all due caution as became the fabulous, but actually seen by Mr. Joseph Thomson, and finally immortalised in fiction, I presume, as the foundation in fact of "King Solomon's Mines."

which they prepare for smoking in the following abominable manner. Their custom is to gather the green leaf, and, without any attempt at drying it, to pound it in a mortar. When sufficiently pounded, the tobacco is made up into balls about the size of a man's fist, and is then dried in a kind of open-work tray hanging in the smoke above the fire of the hut, where, indeed, they constantly keep it until required for use. As they are not at all particular as to the cleanliness of the operation, the tobacco so prepared generally gains from the mortar, in which palm-nuts have probably been pounded, as well as from contact with other substances, to say nothing of the smoke, several flavours which render its use disgusting to Europeans.

Their preparation of wild yams is better worth recording. In the belief that the wild yam, "kampoto," contains a poison which can only be expelled by a somewhat elaborate process, the Bakètè first peel the tubers carefully, and cutting them into thin slices, boil them for a considerable length of time. The slices are then removed from the pot and tied in a basket, which is immersed in running water for five days, after which they are considered fit for use. They are generally eaten cold, but if warmed, they become floury like good European potatoes, and they cannot possibly be distinguished from them by the palate if mashed in orthodox fashion with milk, butter, and pepper.

Their preparations of cassava and of salt are also peculiar, and merit some description. With regard to the former the Bakètè have three methods, of which the following is the most usual:—The manioc roots being freed from the outer bark, are placed in open-work baskets, and sunk in a swiftly running stream for several days, until the cassava has become quite soft and perfectly white. When removed from the water, the roots are generally covered with leeches, and emit a peculiar sour smell, as if fermentation had taken place. So far the process is uniform and uni-

POUNDING CASSAVA.

versal throughout the Congo State, but what follows is, I believe, peculiar to the Bakètè and Baluba. The wet roots are then placed in an open-work tray hanging in the smoke above the hut-fire, and are there kept until perfectly dry and hard, when they are stored away for use as required.

Another method for immediate use is precisely identical with that described above as used in the preparation of wild yams, while the third process is as follows:—The manioc roots being freed from the bark, are rasped down into a kind of coarse flour, which is then dried upon heated stones. The cassava thus obtained closely resembles sawdust in appearance, and is stored away in bags until required. This form of preparation has been, by-the-bye, adopted by the Portuguese on the coast, and the cassava thus prepared goes by the name of *farinha de manioc;* but it is not used by them in the same manner as by the natives, who make it into a kind of porridge. Salt is thus procured:—A kind of floating grass, Chissèngenéné, to be obtained in lagoons and near the edge of very slowly flowing rivers, is collected, and being dried and burned to ashes, the lye thus obtained is mingled with the ashes of a leaf resembling that of the marsh-mallow: these are then mixed with water and set on to boil, the mixture being constantly stirred and skimmed until the water has been gradually evaporated. The sediment remaining is a grey-coloured salt, which amongst the Bakòté and Bakuba is packed dry into large sausage-shaped cases made of leaves, while with the Baluba it is made up *wet* into conical cakes and subsequently dried in the smoke. The salt thus obtained has a disagreeable acrid taste.

The cooking utensils of the Bakòté are peculiar to themselves. The generality of native Congo pottery is thin, not exceeding quarter inch in thickness; but the Bakòté make their large cooking-pots fully half an inch thick, deep also, and with flat bottoms, whereas those of other tribes are rounded underneath.

Their other domestic arts are not in any way remarkable, but their villages are neatly built and well kept. Of canoes they have none, at least, of their own manufacture, and as a rule they eschew piscatory arts and all employments which would necessitate their entering the water. Such fish as they require either for use or barter they purchase from the Bakuba or Baluba fishermen.

As for domestic animals, they keep only goats, sheep, and dogs; the last named being used for hunting, and as good a breed as I have seen anywhere in Africa. The Bakété keep, however, neither pigs nor oxen. Against the former they have a strong prejudice; the latter would be unlikely to thrive in their country, though they sometimes buy oxen in order to slaughter them for food. Cats are unknown: as a consequence house-mice swarm. The Bakété rear large numbers of fowls and ducks, both for their own consumption and for barter, but neither geese nor turkeys, which are a species of fowl unknown to the natives of Central Africa. Upon the whole, I found that we had every reason to congratulate ourselves at Luebo on our proximity to these people, whom I was able to employ in a variety of ways, and to trust as it would have been dangerous to trust few indeed of the native tribes. They were in every sense excellent neighbours and kind friends, and well-wishers to the European State.

To return to our building operations in the new station, it is pleasant to be able to record the progress we had made by Christmas-tide. The new magazine being constructed upon those principles of building adapted to the country, and usually pursued in it, and having taken the trouble to draw proper plans and to make working drawings before beginning to build, we had little or no hindrance to our progress, and by Christmas-day had the satisfaction of dining in the nearly finished storehouse. It measured 60 feet in length by 28 feet in width, with side walls about 14 feet in height, and had a steep widely overhanging roof of thatch rising to a ridge about 36 feet above the ground, supported by a row of central poles. The ends of the building were gabled and pierced with four narrow slits, two above the level of the eaves and two below. On the sides there was in front a central door with a good-sized window on either hand; behind there were two windows: the windows being all protected with stout vertical bars of wood. The materials employed for the walls were wood and clay. Solid upright posts were placed closely together and united by cross-pieces nailed horizontally, and by the wall-plate upon which the rafters rested. These posts were covered to a depth of four inches on both sides with well-worked clay, laid on in two coats, and in the interior finished with a thin wash of the same, its delicate pink colour having a warm and comfortable look. Externally the walls were rough-cast (or "harled," as they call it in Scotland) with a mixture of clay and coarse sand, and white-washed.* The floor of the building (about two feet higher than the ground outside) consisted of well-beaten clay. It was a thoroughly solid, substantial, and sightly building, never giving us any trouble: useful not only for its primary purpose as a storehouse, but available for many an emer-

---

* For this purpose a kind of pipeclay found in small quantities on the Bakètè side of the Lulua was used.

gency. Our clearings had progressed also. All the jungle along the bank of the Luebo throughout the whole length of the station and for 150 yards beyond had vanished; the lagoon was altogether denuded of its surrounding bush; while on the side of the Lulua, from the old road down to the river for about 200 yards, the wood had been cleared away. Thus we were circumstanced when Christmas came to us in our isolation; but though all surrounding nature conspired to banish the wonted associations of the festival, we contrived to remember it, and to celebrate it, at least after a fashion. The workpeople all received a holiday, extra rations, and some presents, and in the evening they had a dance, which was attended by our Bakòtè neighbours, including, of course, several of the fair sex. I must, I fear, in characterising the performance, employ a phrase of Mungo Park's, applied by him to the dances in vogue some eighty years ago in another part of Africa: "The gestures were more voluptuous than elegant." Fortunately for our mess, I had not only a little store of champagne and other European wines, so that we could duly toast our absent friends, but in the morning we had received a very acceptable present of elephant-beef from a Chiplumba-Baluba chief, Kappasiero, who had been out hunting in our neighbourhood. We were unfortunate in the matter of plum-pudding; perhaps not altogether so unfortunate as the legendary English governess, who supplied her French Principal with a recipe from which all mention of the essential cloth in which the pudding must be boiled was omitted, and, in consequence, witnessed the service of a nauseous mess in a soup-tureen as "blum boudin;" yet we were distinctly unfortunate, for though we had most of the ingredients, and did not forget the cloth, yet somehow our recipe was at fault, and the result was an unwholesome soupy affair, chiefly consumed by the cook. We spent, nevertheless, upon the whole, a very pleasant evening inaugurating the new storehouse by our Christmas-dinner, and afterwards witnessing the grotesque dances of the natives in the station clearing, a large bonfire supplying the revellers with quite as much light as was desirable.

Our Christmas festivity over, we settled down again into our usual routine uninterruptedly for a few days. The daily life of a station might be monotonous if the duties of one's office did not so entirely engross all one's thoughts and energies. At Luebo our time and work were apportioned as follows:—5.30 A.M., réveillé; 6 A.M., roll-call, when all the people employed on the station must be present, and when the day's tasks are allotted, tools issued, and working parties told off. At 6.45 A.M., Zanzibari drill until 8 A.M., when we relieved guard and hoisted flag. The men who had been on guard then went off duty for twenty-four hours, being, however, detailed for station cleaning, &c., in the afternoon. I may here remark that of the guard, consisting of six men, four were always off sentry duty, but found occupation in cleaning arms in the guard-house. After going round the station, and attending to my books and reports, I breakfasted at 10.30 A.M. At 12 noon the bugle-call went for the men's dinner, for which two hours were allowed. At 2 P.M. the men were mustered again, and any necessary re-allotment of tasks was then made. From 2 P.M. until 4 P.M. I gave daily audience to all chiefs and others who wished to see me. It may be asked, since many of these persons came considerable distances, what form, in the way of refreshments, my official hospitality assumed. The answer is a simple one. My guests invariably brought with them gourds of palm-wine as a present to me: these I graciously permitted them to consume at once, and upon the premises. At 4 P.M. I went the rounds, inspecting what had been done or not done. This inspection I generally contrived to get through by 5.30 P.M. At 5.45 retreat bugle sounded, when all tools issued in the morning were taken in and counted. Work was completely ended by 6 P.M., when all natives and strangers had to leave the station, unless invited there or detained by special command. At 6.30 P.M. I dined. At 8.30 P.M. first post of tattoo sounded, and at 9 P.M. last post. At 9.30 bugle sounded lights out. My personal arrangements and hours I need not detail, but some further general items may be interesting. Guard was turned out and inspected at 8 A.M., mid-day, retreat, and last post. On Sundays no working parties were detailed, and the men generally went to Kassèngé or elsewhere to make such purchases as they chose; and on Saturdays from 2 P.M. the men had their time to themselves, and the rations were paid in cowries. Monthly on the day of the new moon the Zanzibaris were permitted to hold their saturnalia, but I put a stop to the usual gun-firing, and I persistently declined to *give* them the customary sacrificial goat, though I never refused to sell them one at a sufficient price. Courts-martial I always held on Sundays, and kept prisoners—when unhappily there were any—for trial then, as I had more time to attend to their accusations on that day than on others.

I have made mention of Sunday. It is a day of the week, of course, in Africa as it is in Europe, and we observed it as a holiday—I wish I could say that we observed it as a holy day, but I cannot. Of a certain African town,* where there is a civilised and nominally Christian population, to say nothing of a strong European element, the most exact and unimpeachably accurate of African travellers † says:—"In a central position in the town is a tastefully arranged public garden, *where a band performs on Sunday evenings.* The only public buildings are a well-constructed custom-house, a very good hospital, the house of the governor, a courthouse, *and a church, which is never opened except for baptisms and burials.*" If such be the outward state of religion in those places where there are churches and clergy, we of the laity, located where there are no churches, and in wilds that the clergy of no Christian denomination whatsoever think it worth their while to visit, may, I trust, be pardoned if we do not succeed in making a fairer show in the matter of observances.

On the 31st of December, in the afternoon, Dr. Wolf suddenly returned from Luluaburg. He came to us expressly at this time in order that we might begin the new year together amid good-fellowship and mutual congratulations. This was extremely kind of him: an instance of that thoughtful encouragement of his fellow-workers of which numerous proofs were never wanting. He brought us some additional stores—luxuries, I might call them—but his purpose in visiting Luebo was to embark on board the *En Avant* for an exploration of the Sankoro above its confluence with

* Benguela. † Cameron.

A FATAL ACCIDENT.

the Kasaï. He lost no time, therefore, in departing down the river, bidding us farewell on the 4th of January 1886, both Messrs. Schneider and Vander Felson accompanying him. Thus, after Dr. Wolf's departure, I was alone, but I found full employment in further building operations, as well as in the ordinary routine of administration. He had expressed himself more than satisfied with the progress that had been made, and I was anxious still more to surprise him when he should return.

One tragic event occurred some two months after Dr. Wolf had left us, which varied, in an awful way indeed, our quiet station life. A number of young women belonging to the station were in the habit of bathing at the point where the Lulua and Luebo join. This I had forbidden, as the river abounds with alligators, and had even been at the pains to sketch one of the girls pursued by an alligator, in order to assist my imperfect Siketi in personally dehorting the delinquents from

KAFINGA—A PORTRAIT.

their dangerous amusement. One day, however, in March, in spite of all I could say or do, some of these girls were disporting themselves in the water. I being informed of this little rebellion, went in their direction to order them ashore. All came out except Kafinga—the very girl whose portrait I had sketched—a bright, cheerful creature. She was the farthest out from shore, and was laughingly maintaining her liberty, when, in an instant, uttering a piercing shriek, she disappeared beneath the water. Momentarily forgetful of the alligators, I sprang after the hapless girl, but in vain: indeed, I had drifted some distance down the stream, and was in no small danger myself, when I was picked up by some of my Zanzibaris, who had instantly put off in a canoe to my rescue. Afterwards the natives remembered the strange coincidence of the portrait, and considered the tragedy as a piece of witchcraft, in which I had played a leading, but not altogether enviable, part.

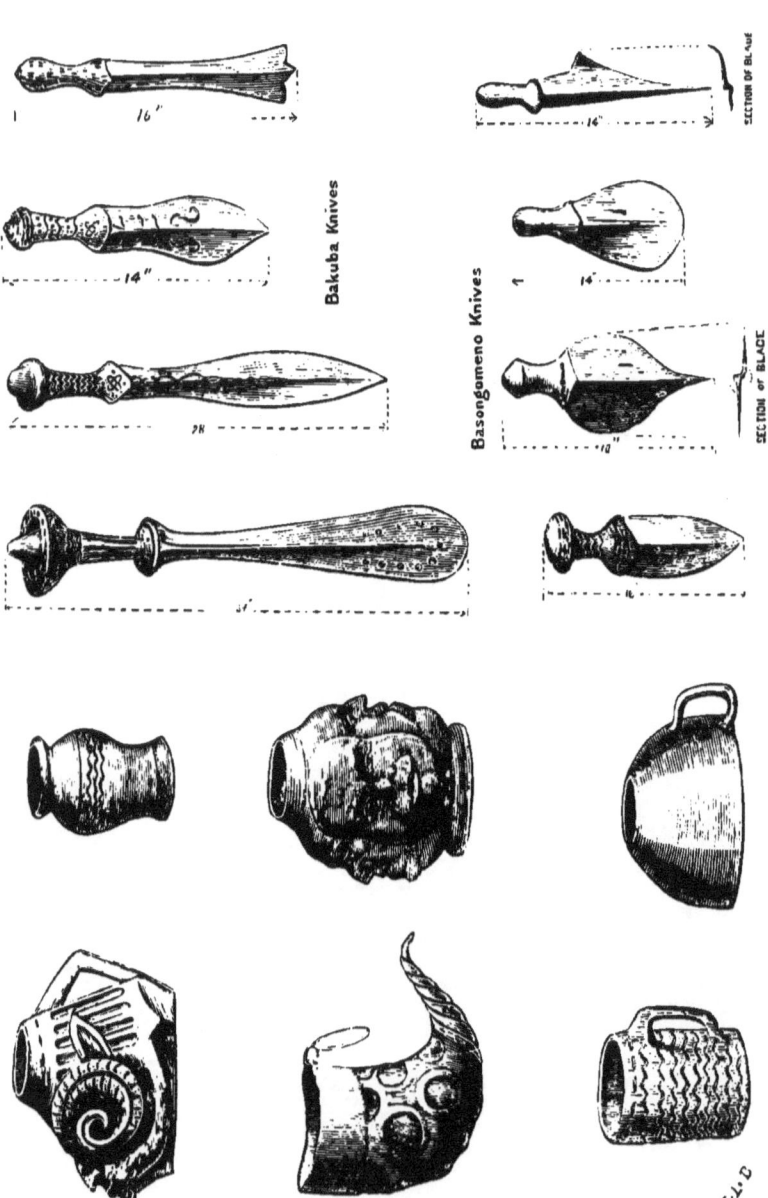

BAKUBA CUPS AND KNIVES.

ZINGAS.

CHAPTER VI.

Portuguese traders—Senhores Saturnino, Carvalho, y Custodio—Their history and trade—Custodio's advice to Dr. Poggé—Carvalho's letter—The partner's application at Luebo—Saturnino and the Zingas—The dispute arranged—Zingas and their country—Progress of the station buildings—The Krupp howitzer—Dr. Wolf's return and the results of his voyage—An agreeable (?) surprise.

DURING Dr. Wolf's absence, a Portuguese, Senhor Saturnino da Souza-Machado, had come into the station from Kapuku on the Muansangoma, where he with a partner had been residing some time for purposes of trade. He came in answer to a reply which I had made to a business inquiry addressed to me by his partner, Senhor Carvalho, whose personal acquaintance I subsequently made. As Senhor Carvalho's history is far from uninteresting in itself, and his trade ventures and adventures both typical of what is, and has been, going on in the way of business in Central Africa, and also in many ways instructive, I shall make a digression in order to acquaint my readers with them.

Born in Portugal, in the province of Las Minas, of humble parentage, Senhor Antonio Lopes de Carvalho emigrated to the Brazils in the capacity of clerk or assistant to his uncle, who was engaged in business there as a coffee-planter and general merchant. After some years spent in the neighbourhood of Rio de Janeiro, Senhor Carvalho was induced to go to Benguela, on the south-west coast of Africa, in the same office as he had held under his uncle. Not meeting with much success as an agent for others, and seeing, at the expiry of years, but small prospect of advancement from his subordinate position, he determined to start business on his own account. In this undertaking he was assisted by a legacy from some relative, wherewith purchasing, partly on credit, a stock of cotton cloth, salt, brass rods, beads, and other small articles of barter, and taking with him a sufficient number of porters lent by his old employer, Senhor Custodio da Souza-Machado, from whom he had obtained his stock, Senhor Carvalho started for the interior. He met with Matjambo (the Mata Yafa, by-the-bye, of Lieut. Cameron) on passing through the Bailunda territory, and experienced not only fair, but even kind treatment from that chief. Senhor Carvalho, however, believing that Matjambo wished to overreach, and use him for his own purposes, refused the chief's solicitations that he would stay with him, and allow the Bailunda to negotiate the exchange of his merchandise for ivory. Accordingly he left Matjambo, and turning more towards the north, passed close to Kassèmbé : thence he journeyed towards Lake Moëro, where he had heard there was abundance of ivory. On this portion of his journey he spent some time, living much as a native, and encountering many adventures, in one of which he came across Dr. Livingstone. He procured as much ivory as he desired, but without having to go so far as the lake, and started on his return. Before reaching Ulundu, however, he was attacked by marauders, robbed of all his ivory, and left practically destitute. He then fled to his friend Matjambo, who received him in all kindness and hospitality, and willingly undertook to maintain him while striving to recover his stolen property. Failing success after some months spent in the attempt, Matjambo generously supplied his guest with means to return to Malange, whither he accordingly departed. He arrived in safety, but destitute, and even considerably in debt to Senhor Custodio, whose service he now re-entered. Some time after Senhor Carvalho's return, the German expedition under Dr. Poggé and Lieut. Wissmann arrived at Malange from Europe. Those gentlemen intended to cross the continent, traversing the Lake Moëro district, and exploring as far as possible the waters of the Kasaï and Sankoro, the existence of which Livingstone had reported. They were induced, however, by the representations partly of Senhor Custodio, to modify their proposed line of march, and eventually they, or at least Lieut. Wissmann, crossed the continent considerably to the north of Lake Moëro, Dr. Poggé returning sick from the

Baluba country to Malange *en route* for Loanda, where he died. In the meantime, Senhor Saturnino, a half-brother of Senhor Custodio's, entering into partnership with Senhor Carvalho, determined to set off in the wake of the expedition, and, by availing himself of it as a pioneer-guard, to introduce a considerable quantity of merchandise into the Baluba country, whose resources had been magnified at Malange by the Matchioko, and thus to establish a permanent trading station in the interior by seizing upon the advantage of being the first to enter the newly opened country. They accordingly departed, taking with them a large stock of goods, representing an outlay of several thousand pounds sterling. Crossing the Upper Luangi, they separated, Senhor Carvalho following that river for a short distance, and striking into the Tucongo country, a land unknown to us save as the abode of ferocious tribes, while Senhor Saturnino proceeded on his way towards the Baluba. Senhor Carvalho lost much from the hostility of the natives, and met with many reverses, but being able nevertheless to hold on his course, he at length came to the Kasaï, crossing which stream, and entering the Bashilangé-Baluba country, he there rejoined Senhor Saturnino. They proceeded to establish themselves on the Muansangoma, where they built a store and dwelling-house combined, and continued to transact business with the natives with varying success. This trade, an unostentatious species of slave-dealing, I will explain. Their *modus operandi* was as follows. Finding it impossible to obtain ivory from the Bakuba or Bakété without exchanging slaves, they purchased from the Baluba slaves of that or kindred races in exchange for cloth, which was valueless to the Bakuba, whose requirements their own excellent native manufacture more than sufficed. The price of a slave would be six yards or under of the cotton cloth or calicôt used in West African commerce, an utterly worthless fabric, value in England less than one penny per yard. The slaves so obtained were passed on to the Bakuba or Bakètè, together with other goods, in exchange for ivory. As a sample of the value given and received, I submit the following statement from original and authentic memoranda in my possession. In return for one slightly damaged "point of ivory" (*apunta avariada custon o' seguinte*) Senhor Carvalho gave—

Duas nymphas	Two young girls.
Cinqua cruzetas de cobra . . .	Five crosses of copper.
Cinqua mil buzio	5000 cowries.
Duas centos bagos d'almandrilha .	200 twisted Venetian beads.

The special iniquity of this trade lies in the fact that slaves purchased by the Bakuba and some similar tribes are upon occasions devoted to death as human sacrifices by their owners. This traffic continued until Senhores Saturnino y Carvalho had gained possession of all the available ivory in that part of the country. They then heard that there was an abundance of ivory still procurable in the country frequented by the Batua Bankonko, whither they therefore temporarily removed. There, for a time, their business prospered; but having quarrelled with the natives for some cause unexplained to me, their encampment was suddenly attacked in the early morning, about thirty of their followers were slain, and they had to make a sudden retreat to Kapuku *viâ* Kabào, where they eventually arrived in a somewhat impoverished and dilapidated condition. Senhor Carvalho thus describes in a letter to me the latter portion of their return journey, in which they endeavoured to retrieve, or at least mitigate, their losses by doing a little business on the road :—

"From Kabâo eight days brought us to the northern frontier of the Bashilangé territory, where we entered that of the Babinji, which we crossed in three days, arriving at the Lubuije, one of the largest affluents of the Lubudi. After we had crossed the former river we began to notice that the aborigines were far from well disposed: they robbed us of various articles, including a bag of cowries, matchets, &c. Unfortunately not one of our carriers or slaves had his gun loaded, so we were unable to give the thieves a lesson before they hid themselves in the thick jungle. For this we had to thank Saturnino's *economia*, which forbade his giving as much as a single cartridge to a servant. Immediately on pitching camp, however, I served out five cartridges to each rifle, yet to obtain this trivial armament I had to go through quite an altercation with Saturnino, for he had not yet profited by our recent experiences. It was now necessary to move forward in regular order of march, on which account one of us conducted the vanguard, the other the rear, between which the whole caravan marched close together. Saturnino remaining a short time after we left camp, was mobbed and instantly deprived of his cap. He carried his rifle indeed, but owing to his mean carefulness it was enclosed in its case, and he had therefore just to put up with the insult. The natives became more and more hostile, and being armed to the teeth, constantly alarmed us by appearing suddenly in our midst, and, with the fleetness of deer, as quickly disappearing in the enclosing bush. I cannot understand anything more disagreeable, as indeed it is impossible to imagine anything more dangerous, than the march through a hostile country along a winding jungle-path, in which the view does not extend beyond a dozen paces. At 3 P.M. we encamped in a small clearing in unfortunate proximity to some predatory villages, whose inhabitants were yet more audaciously thievish than the people who had harassed us on the march. Here the thefts were of momentary occurrence: one would carry off a knife, another a jug from before our very eyes, and another some other article, so that we were greatly embarrassed. By 5 P.M. the natives thronged on all sides and blocked the road, but happily the night passed without any noteworthy circumstance occurring. Next day some natives brought in ivory tusks which they desired to sell, but so exorbitant were their demands as to price, that not all our merchandise would have sufficed to effect a purchase. From this spot, however, we were strangely enough permitted to depart, and to journey for three days without molestation. On arriving at Lakombi, a very populous place, we encountered renewed hostility from the natives, for here, as the saying is, they 'cut our beard for us' (*fazemos nossa barba*), and we had to turn back. On the morning after our arrival, the savages, fully a thousand strong, attacked us, and we were obliged to defend ourselves; but in the course of half an hour, during which the fight lasted, we had four men killed and many wounded. We immediately began our retreat, and camped for the first night in a small open plain. Continuing our journey homewards, we were attacked on the third day from Lakombi by a new foe in the shape of small-pox. This sickness caused many of our loads to be abandoned, and we arrived on the Muansangoma having sustained a loss of about a thousand milreis."

As these merchants had luckily left an ample reserve of goods at their permanent trading station at Kapuku, their losses were limited to the stock they had taken into the Batua Bankonko country, and they were consequently enabled to continue their trade, Senhor Carvalho going for a time to the southward, where he was not unprosperous. The difficulty which now beset the partners was how to get their ivory down to the coast in safety. Being acquainted with the establishment of the station at Luebo, Senhor Carvalho wrote to me inquiring whether we could or would facilitate the transmission of his ivory to the coast by water-carriage *viâ* Léopoldville. To him I replied that we could assume no responsibility as to the goods, but that we certainly would send them as desired if delivered to us at Luebo.

It was in answer to this communication that Senhor Saturnino came into the station, arriving on the day following that on which poor Kafinga had met her awful death; and I shall never forget his coming, for not only was I depressed by the most lively recollections of that dreadful occurrence, but the wetting I had undergone resulted in a night of fever and ague which had so prostrated me that I was disinclined for business of any kind. In addition to the matter about which he had come, Senhor Saturnino had a complaint to prefer against the people of a Bakètè village, whom he represented as having threatened to rob him—in fact, had I not acted most strictly upon Dr. Wolf's general instructions, I should have committed a serious blunder, and greatly injured those very interests which the Free State exists to promote, for I afterwards discovered that Senhor Saturnino's complaint was little better than a malicious fabrication. Being in need of cloth for the pay, and cowries for the rations of my Zanzibaris, I availed myself of Senhor Saturnino's visit to purchase a small supply of those articles from him, of course at extravagant prices. He started on his return journey the same day as he arrived, being, or professing to be, in a state of nervous apprehension as to the attitude of the Bakété, and I gave him such protection as I deemed fit, that is to say, an escort of six Zanzibaris with a corporal. On their return journey they convoyed a number of Senhor Saturnino's Zingas bearing the goods I had purchased from him. These poor fellows, seeing the happier life our people led, absolutely refused to return to their master, and insisted on volunteering for service under the State. On hearing of this, their compatriots still in Senhor Saturnino's service forthwith, for the most part, forsook him, and came to me, so that, as I enlisted them readily enough, my force was raised to about one hundred men. These proceedings, which I at once notified to Senhor Saturnino, brought us into renewed communication, and eventually his partner, Senhor Carvalho, came to Luebo in no very amiable frame of mind. He represented that not only were the enlisted Zingas indebted to him for thefts of his goods committed at various times, but that they were bound by a contract, concluded at Malange in due form before the Commandant of that place, in virtue of which they must remain in his service for an indefinite period at a stipulated remuneration, not to be paid until their return to Angola, and for rations which were to be supplied to them from time to time, and he produced papers in support of his contention. What he did *not* state was that the head chief of these men had practically sold them to Senhor Saturnino, for he had agreed that none of his people taking service under the partners should return to their homes unless accompanied by one or other of their masters, or unless bringing proof of their decease, and that should any of the Zingas return otherwise, they were to be most severely punished—practically put to death. On the other hand, I explained to Senhor Carvalho, and demonstrated by documentary evidence, that the laws of the Congo State did not recognise as binding contracts made by "third parties," because people, to be personally and individually bound by a contract, must personally and individually consent to the same, and to that end must understand and be in every way cognisant of the whole conditions of the contract. I then caused the men to be interrogated upon the subject, and found that they had most certainly not committed themselves to the contract, and that being all free men, and not slaves (some of them were petty chiefs), their head chief had acted *ultra vires* in contracting for them. At the same time I examined into the alleged thefts, some of which the Zingas acknowledged. Accordingly I informed Senhor Saturnino that excepting a few individuals whom he had expressly asked me not to engage, and whom I referred back to him, I was prepared to retain the enlisted Zingas, and to keep back from their pay the amount of their debts to him, for

ZINGAS AND THEIR COUNTRY.

which I gave him a cheque. I have every reason to believe that the merchant was as ill pleased with the settlement as I was satisfied, for the Zingas almost without exception turned out excellent and trustworthy workmen.

Although the Zinga country does not lie within the limits of the Congo State, nor yet immediately contiguous to its boundaries, those people are so frequently to be met with in that part of the Congo territory which I am describing, that I shall make a digression in order to give a brief account of them. In former days they were a powerful nation under the rule of queens, whose dominion extended as far north as the mouth of the Congo. Commercial treaties, however, with the Portuguese have so greatly curtailed their boundaries that the Zinga country does not now extend farther north than the Kwanza, and is, in fact, a district some fifty miles square extending along that river. The nation is now wholly tributary to the Portuguese, its internal government being practically in the hands of the head chief or chiefs, and the queen's supremacy has shrunk to a mere *nominis umbra*. The Zingas are a fine athletic race and brave; good workmen and faithful servants when in an alien country. They bring no women with them, but marry those of the country in which they may be sojourning. With their own native institutions I have no acquaintance, as they adopted the manners of the people with whom they dwelt.

So large an accession to our numbers enabled me to make much more rapid progress with our station clearings and buildings than before. By this time I had completed the central store and the dining pavilion on the Point —the latter an octagonal structure built on the same principles as the central store, but open on all sides above 3 feet 6 inches from the ground, and fitted with curtains of matting, two sides being entirely open down to the ground. The floor was not properly finished until a much later date, when it, together with all the more important floors in the station, were paved with fine hard tiles made by one of the Angolese: meantime it was made of well-beaten clay. The palisades along both river fronts were completed, and the ramping was in progress. The kitchen and cook's dwelling-house were rather more than half finished, and the land approach to the station was temporarily palisaded. The bastion at the Point, which I had designed with the object of placing a gun (Krupp No. 1 mountain howitzer, 5.7 calibre) upon it in such position as to enfilade both river fronts, was by this time finished, and had proved a most laborious undertaking, as its base and lower stage had to be built up with the largest masses of stone we could contrive to move. Another tedious piece of stone-work in progress at this time was the embankment outside the palisade next the Luebo, which we were obliged to construct in order to protect the station site against the stream, whose force was gradually but surely eating it away. With the increased number of workmen I made rapid progress in clearing the jungle towards the south, so as to gain room for our plantations, and in making the road towards Luluaburg. Thus when Dr. Wolf returned from the Sankoro he found many changes and improvements in the condition of the station.

The exploration of the Sankoro is so far a portion of my own narrative, that my lack of ability to recount its precise

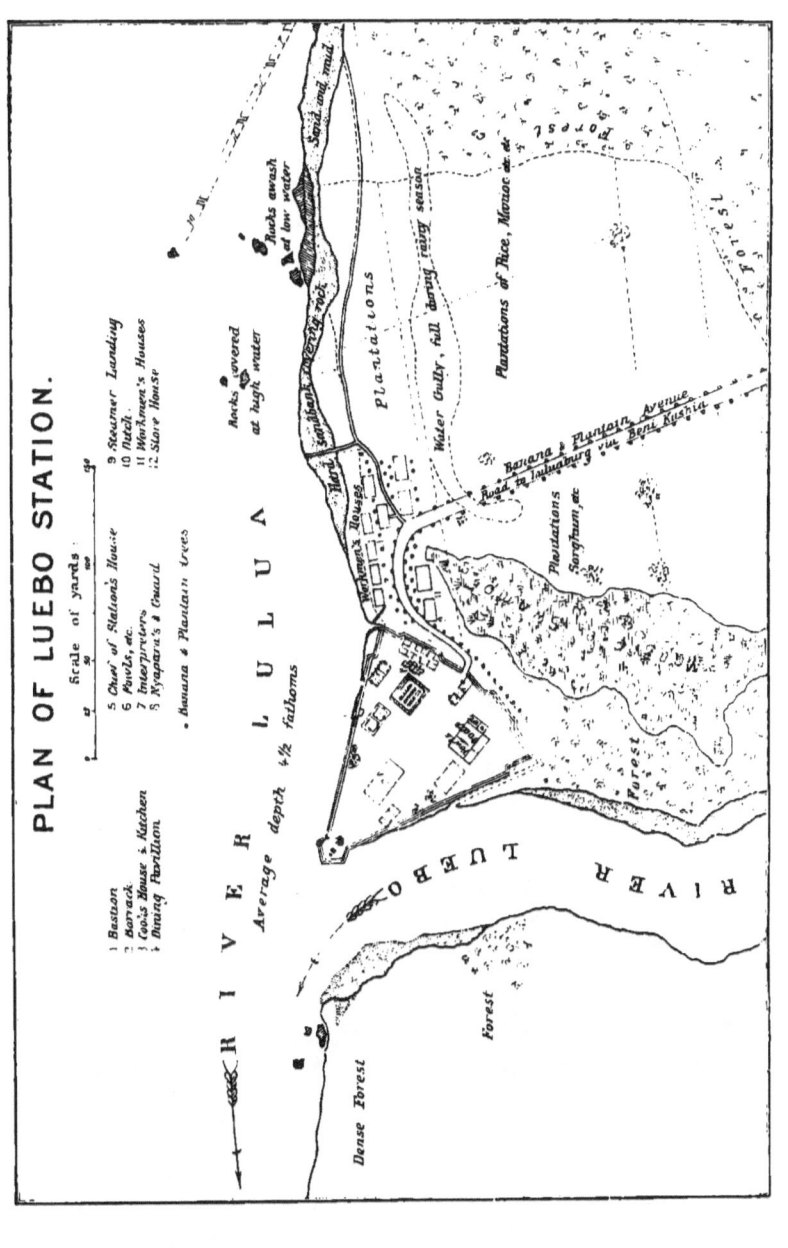

details will not void my liability to tell the leading incidents of the story as they were told to me. After descending the Kasaï to its junction with the Sankoro, and thence ascending the latter a short distance, the *En Avant* met with a slight accident, which was soon repaired. The expedition then voyaged up the river for about a week before coming into communication with the natives, whom they found very shy. Proceeding farther, they entered the dominions of a chieftainess, who received the party in a most friendly way, and with whom they remained two or three days. The expedition next encountered some danger from predatory natives, when by mischance the *En Avant* had run upon a sandbank.* The greater part of the goods had to be taken out of the vessel, and the cloth and various articles of wearing apparel were spread abroad to dry. The natives observed with envy so great a display of wealth, and deeming it to be quite undefended—for the members of the expedition being unprovided with arrows, were in their opinion unarmed—they determined to possess themselves of it. They, however, committed the additional error of supposing their language utterly unknown to their intended victims, for happening to discuss the project in the presence of Humba, the interpreter, they inadvertently apprised him of their design. He immediately informed Dr. Wolf, who was accordingly on his guard. During a palaver which he held with the chief, Dr. Wolf, in order to prove that he possessed a more potent weapon than bows and arrows or spears,

---

* Just at this juncture it was discovered that the fire-bars in the engine furnace were burnt through. Mr. Schneider made use of two rifle-barrels wherewith to repair the damage during this interruption to the voyage.

fired off a barrel of his revolver in the air, making as little premonitory movement as possible. The effect on the natives may be more easily imagined than described: in the wildest alarm they rushed to their canoes, capsizing many in their frantic efforts to escape in them, and fled headlong in every direction. Proceeding yet farther, the expedition came to parts where the natives were more friendly and reliable, and not far from the junction of the Lomami with the Sankoro, Dr. Wolf met with the renowned ivory and slave trader Sappoo Sahib, who with a large armed retinue, chiefly of Arabs and Nyamweze, chanced to be in that part of the country on a trading excursion. Dr. Wolf was much pleased with his manner and appearance, which he described as dignified and courteous. He is a Mohammedan, of course, and is generally held as the second great marauder-merchant of Central Africa; Tippoo Tib being, since the overthrow of Mirambo, *facile princeps*. Passing the mouth of the Lomami, the expedition ascended the Sankoro, which they found interrupted with rapids. These surmounted, others were encountered, up which it was impossible to take the *En Avant*, for although there appeared to be sufficient depth of water, the steam power of the boat was unequal to the task. From this point, not far short of 320 miles from its confluence with the Kasaï, the Sankoro was descended as far as the Lomami, the ascent of which Dr. Wolf next attempted. Rapids, however, again barred the way at no great distance above its mouth, and the expedition had to turn back and regain the Sankoro. The remainder of the descent was entirely uneventful, and the whole excursion may be regarded as most fortunate. The

RESULTS OF THE EXPLORATION.

exploration had resulted in the discovery of some 400 miles of inland navigation, extending through a rich and fertile country, in which, wherever the banks were wooded, there was abundant evidence of the existence of elephants, and where the natives consequently were possessed of no small store of ivory. But the most important result was the demonstration that the united waters of the Lomami and Sankoro discharge themselves into the Congo, together with those of the Kasaï and Kwango, at Kwamouth, and not independently either by the Lubiranzi or Buruki, as had been supposed. How far the success of this expedition was due to Dr. Wolf's prudence and indomitable perseverance, or to mere good fortune, those who have served on exploring expeditions in Africa can best determine. The results of so much courage, toil, and anxiety read lightly as the record of a pleasant summer trip, but those who have taken part in the living reality can feel how easily the expedition might have ended otherwise. Many, if not all, the circumstances attending it would—*me judice*—with almost any other man in command, have led to failure : with Dr. Wolf they formed the basis of success.

The return of the *En Avant* was attended by an amusing incident at Luebo, which, as it is a tale that points a moral, may be worth recounting. For the same reason, and since it illustrates the same maxim, a legend that has long been current in my own family shall also be narrated. And the moral of both is this : never attempt a pleasant surprise unless you are quite sure that the surprise to your friends may not merely fail of its pleasant character, but may eventually prove an unpleasant surprise to yourself. Many years ago, when the Church of the United Brethren was a flourishing, though always small religious community in England, a certain worthy single sister was sent thither by the authorities at Herrnhut. The voyage from Hamburg across the North Sea was in those days a long and very tedious affair of perfectly uncertain duration, and the good sister had on this occasion ample time for reflection in the complete solitude in which she found herself on board a sailing vessel manned by Englishmen, of whose language she was as ignorant as they were of hers. It naturally occurred to her that the present was a good opportunity of acquiring a little preliminary knowledge of English, with the view of astonishing her friends in London by her rapid acquisition of the national language. Accordingly she observed the crew, listening attentively to their mode of salutation, and practising those words that seemed to be delivered as well with the most cordial good-will as with the greatest force of expression. When at length the vessel, ascending the Thames, moored off the Custom House stairs, and the local brethren came on board to welcome her, the sister's grand opportunity to display her learning and surprise her friends arrived. To their kindly words of greeting and of inquiry the amazing response was given—"Goot morning, tamm your ice!" Horrified at such a salute from one so pious, and by other yet more reprehensible phraseology that followed, the worthy people hastily requested her to speak only in German for the present, and wondered much among themselves why Providence had sent them such a swearing sister. Very similar was the success attending the greeting with which the Sankoro expedition designed to surprise us on their return. It was long after nightfall, and I was sitting in the dining-room on the Point writing, according to my usual custom, when, suddenly through the stillness of the night, above the booming of the rapids, I heard the scream of a shell followed by the report of a gun, and then a crash. Almost immediately the bugler sounded to arms, and before I had time to stay the alarm, every one was rushing here and there in frightened preparation to resist some invisible foe. Just for a moment I myself had wondered who it might possibly be that was shelling us, but, of course, I instantly thought of the *En Avant*, and rejoiced that she had returned. I soon had my people reassured, and beyond the fright that it caused a Zanzibari who chanced to be below the cotton-wood tree into which the shell crashed, this pleasant surprise caused no damage to any one; but its result *might* have been very different. When, next morning, the vessel came up to the station landing-place, about 7 A.M., we learned that on the last day of her voyage, having a rather longer distance to overtake than could be accomplished in daylight, the *En Avant* held on through the darkness until obliged to stop for a supply of wood. They knew that they were not far from the station, but being unaware of their exact position, they deemed themselves at a sufficiently safe distance to permit their surprising us in the charming (?) manner in which they had announced their proximity. We found the *En Avant* laden with curiosities of all kinds: a perfect museum of the countries through which she had passed. Amongst the collection were some singular shields,

G

made of bamboo pith, backed with cowhide, and grotesquely coloured red and white with clay; a number of really beautiful battle-axes inlaid with copper; drinking-cups of wood richly carved, and of quaint design; and native cloth finely woven in patterns so rich and admirably varied that no one could believe it the work of an uncivilised race. Mr. Vander Felson, too, had largely compensated himself for the loss of his valued parrot on the Congo by acquiring a numerous assortment of that species: amongst them a king parrot, gorgeous in his lovely scarlet plumage.

THE HOMAGE OF CONGOLEMOSCH

CHITABO ON MIAW.

CHAPTER VII.

Dr. Wolf attempts to ascend the Kasaï—The *En Avant* disabled—A perilous project—The *Peace* arrives with Lieut. Wissmann on board, and departs towing the *En Avant* down to Léopoldville—Vander Felson's farewell—Wissmann and Wolf go to Luluaburg, and thereafter explore the Kasaï up to its first falls—The *Stanley* arrives at Luebo—Adventure of the Baron de Schwerin—Results of Messrs. Wissmann and Wolf's excursion to the Kasaï—Our journey to Luluaburg—The neighbouring natives—Incidents of the march—Accident at the Miaw—Luluaburg—Congolemosch—Kashia-Calemba and the king—Lubuku and lhiamba-smoking.

Dr. Wolf, who had returned on the 7th of April 1886, did not allow himself any long period of repose. The few days he spent at Luebo were all busily employed in storing and arranging the trophies of discovery, and in making ready the *En Avant* for her next voyage. This, it was settled, should be on the Upper Kasaï, above the junction of the Lulua with that river. Accordingly, as soon as ever arrangements could be made, the *En Avant*, with Dr. Wolf and the same officers and crew on board, unmoored from Luebo and dropped down the stream, bound once more for waters new and unexplored. Gaining the confluence of the rivers, and camping there that night, the expedition began next morning to ascend the Kasaï. They had not, however, gone far before one of the paddles struck against a snag, and so injured itself, and also the engine, that the latter becoming useless, and the pump refusing to work, the *En Avant* floated a helpless log upon the river. Drifting with the stream back again to the mouth of the Lulua, the vessel anchored, and Dr. Wolf immediately ordered the whaleboat to be manned, and provisioned for the ascent of the Kasaï, a feat which he intended thus to undertake, leaving Messrs. Schneider and Vander Felson on board the steamer, with orders to obtain certain stores, and reinforcements from me, and thereafter to attempt to navigate the *En Avant* down-stream, first to Kwamouth, and thence to Léopoldville for repairs. Providentially the courage and energy of Dr. Wolf and his subordinates were not to be subjected to so severe a test, nor were they so far to tempt misfortune. Just as the whaleboat was pushing off, the Baptist missionary steamer *Peace*, with Lieut. Wissmann, the Baron von Nimptsch, Meinheer Greshoff, and the Rev. George and Mrs. Grenfell on board, came in sight. This meeting was as fortunate as it was unexpected, for while it delivered the people of the *En Avant* from their trying situation, it secured for one of the company on board the *Peace* that skilful surgical treatment of which he stood in need. Herr von Nimptsch had somehow come by an ugly wound on his hand, which would probably have rendered amputation necessary had it remained much longer undressed. Taking Dr. Wolf on board, and the whaleboat in tow, the *Peace* came on to Luebo; the *En Avant* being left at the confluence, to be taken down-stream when the party should return. Thus I was agreeably surprised by the arrival of our visitors, though I naturally regretted that disaster should so soon have overtaken the Kasaï exploration.

We took our guests up the Luebo, as far as the navigation permitted, to see the Falls, the only "lion" of the station, except the plantations at Kassèngè, which we also visited. I wonder much whether we really made a more practical use of some of our time in selecting a site for a mission station, in the hope that some day the Baptist Missionary Society might be able to occupy it.

After a sojourn of three days, the *Peace* left us on her return down the Lulua, taking with her the personal effects of Messrs. Schneider and Vander Felson, who had remained on board the *En Avant* at the confluence, and were to go on thence to Léopoldville without returning to Luebo. I sent down by the steamer Mr. Vander Felson's collection of parrots, about which he had written to me. He had kindly said in concluding his note, and with reference to the period which must inevitably elapse before we should see anything of each other again, that he hoped we should "meet on the other side of the water." Poor fellow! he little thought to what water his words would apply. He died at Banana when actually on board the homeward-bound steamer.

The *Peace* took away all the party she had brought except Lieut. Wissmann, who had come back from Madeira recruited in health, and prepared for further exploration. His first work at Luebo was to go through the stores in our magazine, with the view of ascertaining how far they might be available in supplying an expeditionary force to cross the continent to Zanzibar, which should examine *en route* into the existence of the reputed Lake Muatanzigé. Finding that we had at best nothing to spare wherewith to furnish forth an expedition—for the Sankoro exploration had, as a matter of necessity, lessened our store—Lieut. Wissmann, leaving his heavier luggage at Luebo, went on to Luluaburg in company with Dr. Wolf. Thence he passed rapidly to Muansangoma, ordering a good supply of cloth and cowries from Senhor Saturnino, which he divided between the two stations of Luebo and Luluaburg. From Muansangoma he came on direct to Luebo, where Dr. Wolf rejoined him, and they determined to accomplish together that which the latter had essayed in exploring the Upper Kasaï. For that purpose the whaleboat was refitted; a new and improved awning being introduced, and other improvements effected which rendered it more suitable for the accommodation of an exploring party. They took with them eight rowers and a serving boy, together with a small quantity of provisions and all requisites for making observations.

Only a day or two after the departure of this small party the merchandise ordered from Senhor Saturnino reached us. It was convoyed by Senhor Carvalho in person, who continued thenceforward to reside chiefly in the immediate vicinity of the station—at least so long as I remained there—for the purpose of building canoes, and thereby pushing his trade interests amongst the riparian tribes.

In the course of the week following, the *Stanley*, under command of Lieut. Andersson, arrived at Luebo, having on board Captain the Baron de Mácàr and Lieut. Le Marinel, both officers of the Carabineers, who were sent for the purpose of taking over on behalf of the State the station of Luluaburg, which had been heretofore the property of Lieut. Wissmann's expedition. There was also on board the *Stanley* the Baron de Schwerin, envoy of the Swedish Government, who was travelling through the Congo State, with the approbation of the Governor, for purposes of scientific observation. This nobleman encountered an adventure on the evening of the same day on which he arrived at Luebo that might have had a very unfortunate termination. Having been more than fully engaged during the greater part of that day, I had no opportunity of looking after our guests, but on our assembling at 6 P.M. in the dining pavilion, and missing the Baron from the company, I remembered having seen him a little before five o'clock, and having answered a question he had addressed to me as to the distance of the Luebo Falls. As, after waiting for some time, we were obliged to dine without him, we began to fear that he had gone thither, and returning too late, had lost his way, and might be wandering helplessly in the jungle. Accordingly, after dinner, we sent out a search party accompanied by a bugler, but they returned about 10 P.M., their search having proved entirely fruitless. At this juncture Senhor Carvalho volunteered his services, and set out with a fresh party. Their efforts were happily successful. They were so fortunate as to come upon the Baron, who having lost his way, and calmly despairing of recovering it in the darkness, was, with a curious indifference to, or ignorance of, the frightful dangers surrounding him, actually preparing to pass the night in a kind of cubicle that he had made for himself with leaves and branches. When brought into the station, M. de Schwerin was drenched with the heavy rain that had fallen after sunset, and shivering with incipient fever; but timely remedies being administered, no serious consequences supervened, and he was able to continue his observations without any material interruption.

The *Stanley* had spoken the *Peace* with the *En Avant* in tow near the Nzali Mpini, but had seen nothing of Lieut. Wissmann's party at the confluence of the Kasaï and Lulua, which was precisely what we had expected. Before our visitors left us, however, we were surprised by the return of the expedition. It appeared that the Kasaï was navigable for only about forty miles above the embouchure of the Lulua—a much less distance than had been anticipated. The cataracts which interrupted its navigation were, in the lower fall, about twenty-three feet in height, the upper fall having a less elevation. From their position it may be reasonably inferred that the bar of rock here crossing the bed of the Kasaï is identical with that which interrupts the Lulua above its junction with the Luebo, causing, however, in the latter case, a multitude of rapids rather than one or two well-defined cataracts. The expedition made no minor discoveries of a noteworthy character, and its main result—the discovery of the falls, which Lieut. Wissmann named after himself—made it plain that any further exploration of the Kasaï must be undertaken from the shore or in boats carried a greater or less distance overland. In the course of two or three days the *Stanley* discharged her cargo of stores—an ample supply—and having taken on board Dr. Wolf, with his scientific collections, and re-embarked M. de Schwerin, she left us on her return voyage to Léopoldville.

We had now in prospect a journey of about 120 miles to Luluaburg, from which station saddle-oxen for the party had been sent, and had arrived at Luebo some ten days after the departure of the *Stanley*. It was arranged that during my absence Senhor Carvalho should be in charge of the station, and all other preparations having been completed by the 8th of June, Lieut. Wissmann, Mons. de Mácàr, Mons. Le Marinel, and myself, accompanied by a sufficient escort, began our march on the forenoon of that day. Taking the native road through the dense jungle, we followed its winding and uneven course, until, some fourteen miles from Luebo, we came out into open and grassy country, through which we held on for about eight miles farther, where we arrived at the Chiplumba village of Beni-Kashia, situated on the verge of a rapid descent into the forests overhanging the Luebo, to which river it is somewhat nearer than to the Lulua. It is rather a poor place, being exposed to the interference of Shammatuka and Bakèté neighbours, but the chief, Chikabo, met us with seeming courtesy, and made the usual presents. On leaving camp next morning, June 9th, we skirted along the edge of a great landslip, where the ground had gone down a depth of perhaps 300 feet towards the Luebo, the drainage area of which river we here left, crossing the deep-wooded valleys of two small streams flowing independently towards the Lulua. Passing over the north-eastern slopes of a range of low hills, running N.N.E. and S.S.W., we came into the basin of the Musisi, high-lying grass-land through which the river has been for ages deepening its way to the Lulua, so that it now flows at the bottom of a densely wooded ravine, presenting. at the point at which we crossed it, a steep descent of upwards of 700 feet on either side. The Musisi itself we found to be wide though rapid and very shallow, much discoloured by the presence of some kind of yellow earth, and easily fordable. Having crossed and gained the level of the rolling grass-land once more, we camped near the site of a deserted village, where the ruined half-uprooted plantations made the wilderness look doubly desolate. Leaving camp early on the 10th, and proceeding for some five miles through a grassy country, we came to one of the tributaries of the Musisi, running towards the S.W. through a similarly deep and densely wooded glen. The stream itself, known as the Luisi, covering a narrow bed of rock, is rapid, deep in places, and dark-looking. This crossed, we came at mid-day to Beni Muamba, a fair-sized village, or rather collection of villages, situated amid the grassy plain, where we noticed for the first time in our journey the ensign of the Lubuku brotherhood —a worn-out kinshu (hollow gourd for smoking lhiamba) raised on a long pole. The chief received us in the customary manner, and we rested there for luncheon. Proceeding on our way, we came late to the site of another deserted town, about twenty miles from our last camping-ground. Here we halted for the night, and thence made an early start

LOOKING BACK ACROSS THE MUSHI VALLEY.

on the morning of the 11th; but having been unable, of course (owing to the fact that we were in an uninhabited district), to obtain sufficient provisions for our men, we could continue our journey no farther than to Chinyama, where we encamped. As I shall fully describe the country through which we passed on the 11th and following day in giving the details of my return journey, I need only here remark, that before nightfall on the 12th we reached the post on the Miaw river known as Chitabo, which Herr Bugslag, the chief of the station at Luluaburg, had established for the convenience of travellers passing between that station and Luebo: a nice little house just above high-water level at the river's edge. The descent to this stream from the uplands, unlike that of every other considerable river we had crossed in our journey from Luebo, was very gradual and destitute of wood. The road took us through the village, where the chief, Muanamput, having been guilty of some very serious misconduct, received a severe personal correction from Lieut. Wissmann.

The grotesquely ugly name of this place (Miaw) had led me into an amusing mistake some months previously. Having despatched a messenger to Luluaburg, I required from him on his return a circumstantial account of his journey. On asking him where he had slept on the first night after leaving Luluaburg he replied, "Miaw." Thinking that my ears had deceived me, I repeated my question, and received again the same reply, only with more emphasis, "Miaw!" Being now convinced that the man was intending to display his independence by insolently mimicking a cat or some other animal instead of replying to my question, I smartly rebuked him, when, the interpreter happily intervening, the matter was explained.

Of course we encamped for the night at the little house by the river, and were ferried across early next morning. Just below the crossing-place there are some rapids, so diversified and broken with rocks as to present a pleasing bit of water-scenery. The Miaw, in common with all the rivers we had passed, falls into the Lulua, to which it contributes a stream of clear, almost perfectly colourless water. When we crossed in the morning, we found that Gomez, the assistant-interpreter at Luluaburg, had arrived thence the preceding evening with two saddle-oxen for our use, in case those that Lieut. Wissmann and I had ridden should be over-fatigued. Not being informed of his peculiarities, when I came to mount the bullock assigned me, I went through a performance more amusing to the onlookers than to myself. No sooner did I attempt to seat myself on the saddle, than down the brute settled himself on his knees, and as he seemed to mean rolling, I thought it best to make him rise before again trying to mount. This was not so easily to be done: it was only after long and violent efforts on the part of the bullock-man that we succeeded in getting him up. Just as he was rising I sprang upon his back, and making a vigorous use of spurs and whip, contrived to get him properly in hand, after which he gave us no further trouble. Subsequently I was told that the creature had been trained by his former master to this conduct, and had I only placed myself on the saddle at first when he subsided, he would not have rolled, as I had anticipated, but would have risen with me on his back.

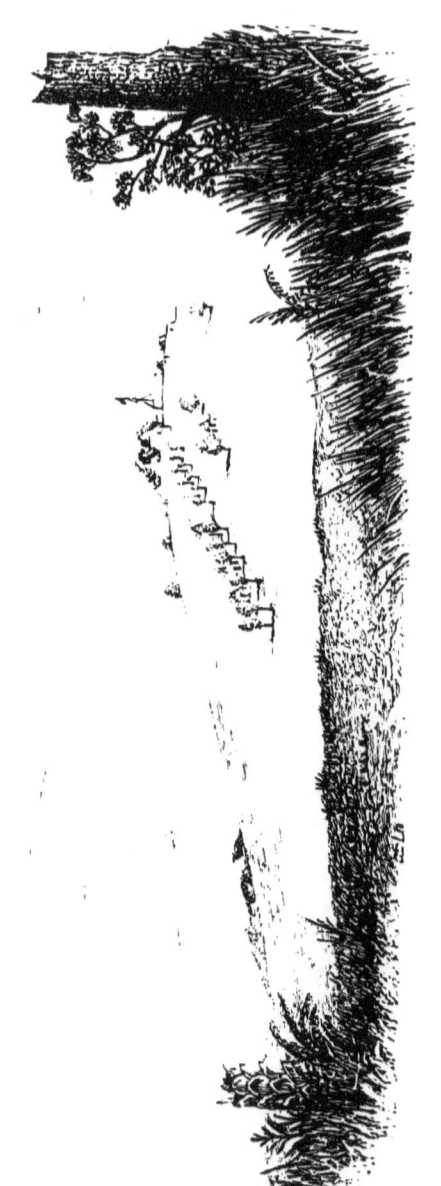

LULLABURG.

(*To face page 104.*)

LULUABURG.

The road still lay through a grassy country gradually rising from the river, from which we had not gone far when a beautiful harness-back antelope bounded across our path, with such speed, that although we were on the look-out for game, which is abundant near these rivers, and fired after it, the creature escaped scatheless. Our party, quite an imposing cavalcade for this part of the country, was an object of wonder and admiration to the inhabitants of the several small villages through which we passed. They had been apprised of our coming, and turned out to salute us with the usual clapping of hands and cries of welcome, so that we drew to the end of our journey in a species of triumph. Soon after mid-day we came to a small stream called the Pioko, in crossing which Lieut. Wissmann had the misfortune to injure his thumb severely with a snap-hook attached to the rein of the bullock which he was riding: one cannot be too careful, in riding these animals, to provide against every possibility of hurt and accident. From this stream we gradually ascended to Luluaburg, seated on the summit of its grass-covered hill, approaching it through a newly planted avenue of manganga trees, and arrived at our destination, where we were received by Herr Bugslag about 2 P.M. on the 13th of June.

Luluaburg crowns the summit of an isolated hill some 400 feet above the Lulua, from which it is distant about a mile. It is fully entrenched and fortified, and besides three dwelling-houses for Europeans, contains two barracks for coloured soldiers and employés, an interpreter's house, and the usual offices of kitchen, &c., and two stores. There is also a house for the women employed about the station, as well as goat, pig, and cattle yards. The plantations cover a large portion of the sloping ground between the station and the river: the beautiful prospect from the dining-room, which looks in this direction—nearly due east—being greatly enhanced by the variety which these cultivated enclosures impart to the fore and middle ground. All the hilly country visible from Luluaburg is almost bare of trees, being wooded only in the lowest valleys, and presents to the eye nothing but a sea of rounded hilltops unbroken by cliffs, crag, or forest. Large herds of cattle, sheep, and goats graze through these downs, those belonging to the station being numerous, and sufficient for its meat supply. When I visited the plantations, they were in admirable order, and are, I am told, a source of profit as well as a great convenience. It was at that time expected that the yield of grain would shortly make the station quite independent of imported supplies of that nature. The climate of Luluaburg is indubitably much more salubrious than that of Luebo: the entire absence of forest and swampy land for many miles around, the great altitude and perfect drainage of the station, and the good water, all unite to make it, for the latitude, an exceptionally healthy place.

The native population in the immediate vicinity of Luluaburg is very considerable, as compared at least with the neighbourhood of Luebo and districts farther down the rivers. Kashia-Calemba, the capital of the Bashilangé-Baluba, is only about $5\frac{1}{2}$ miles distant from the station, and there are other large villages equally near; but our first visit, after a day or two's rest, was paid to a chief on the other side of the Lulua—Congolemosch by name. As our business was to receive, or more correctly to enforce, his submission and homage, we took with us a considerable body of men. This chief, a cousin of Calemba's, had, during the latter's absence down the Congo with Lieut. Wissmann's expedition, conceived the idea of making himself independent of his sovereign, and to this end was embracing every occasion of resisting his authority and of raising disputes. Doubtless he had been irritated by arbitrary conduct on the part of Calemba's representatives, and had withal some solid arguments to urge in his own behalf, but the course which sound policy dictated to us was nevertheless extremely simple. Calemba's authority must be upheld by us in union with our own, which Congolemosch had also defied. Accordingly, on the 15th of June, when we arrived at his village peacefully enough, though accompanied by some 200 armed followers, we came to ascertain from him explicitly whether he would or would not return to his allegiance. Seeing our numbers and arms, he received us with all becoming respect and seeming cordiality, quickly deciding which course he would pursue as to his submission. We had a long but not unpleasant palaver, although the act of homage which ensued, however curious to witness, was anything but gratifying to one's feelings: to me, at least, it is painful to see a human being grovelling in so abject a manner. After protesting his entire devotion and absolute service, poor Congolemosch retired to a distance of some five or six yards from us, and throwing himself down on his face, rolled himself towards Lieut. Wissmann's feet. There he licked the ground with his tongue, and covering his extended hands with dust, raised them in a suppliant manner towards Lieut. Wissmann, who, at this point, lifted him up, and the ceremony came to an end. The tribute for which we had stipulated was afterwards duly paid.

On the morrow we all went to Kashia-Calemba to make our visit of ceremony. Less than an hour's ride along the well-made and perfectly kept road, of an uniform width of forty feet, brought us to our destination, where we were received in the central square of the town by Calemba in person, his sister, Meta Sànkolla (a woman of great intellectual power and force of character), and the principal men. The town may contain a population of about 2500 souls, and is built with some attempt at regularity, though in every way, except in point of size, inferior to the Bakèté and Basongo-Meno towns that I had seen. It is unfortified and unenclosed, standing on the verge of a grassy plain at the summit of an ascent similar to that which leads to Luluaburg. The plantations belonging to the town, from which they are distant about half a mile, are situated on the road by which we had come. The central square is remarkable, as being the place in which burns the perpetual fire, that, together with the custom of Ihiamba or hemp-smoking, has been introduced among the Bashilangé-Baluba by the Matchioko as a species of religion under the name of "Lubuku," *i.e.*, friendship. The sacred fire is constantly fed with logs by the older men and women, who, more or less decrepit, are unable to work much for their living, and being supported by the community at large as a sort of college, occupy the houses assigned them in the square. Besides maintaining the perpetual fire. these old people have to cultivate and prepare the lhiamba for smoking: the *Cannabis Indica*, known in Zanzibar as bhangi or bhang. Apart from such use as may be made of it privately, lhiamba is smoked ceremonially as a token of friendship, and is also administered to accused persons as a species of ordeal. Its public or ceremonial smoking is begun by the chief or senior man present placing the prepared weed in the "kinsu dhiamba" (*i.e.*, lhiamba pipe), and, after smoking a while himself, passing it on to the man next to him. This pipe consists of a small clay bowl, to contain the burning lhiamba, inserted in the larger end of a hollow gourd, the smaller end of which has a large aperture, against which the smoker places

LHIAMBA (*Cannabis Indica*).

his mouth and inhales the smoke in great gulps. In many a naïve town night is made horrible by this hateful practice. Crouching around the glowing fire amid the fitful darkness of a cloudy night, the dusky brethren of Lubuku pass round the intoxicating pipe. Meantime the tom-toms beat their one eternal accompaniment to the wild song in which the smokers join at will, sometimes making rude harmony, and sometimes drowning, by discordant cries, the melody sustained by the less frenzied revellers. Each smokes in turn, and then is shaken, and almost suffocated, by the screaming and unnatural cough that invariably succeeds. As the baneful poison acts upon the brain, a sudden frenzy falls upon the smoker, who, leaping up, pours forth with frantic gestures and loud cries a perfect torrent of incoherent speech. And so, the pipe going round the circle, some are sinking into quietude, while others smoke again or sing, and others rave in madness and delirium, or screech, and choke, and cough in hideous chorus until the poison and exhaustion gain the victory, and, one by one, the revellers sink into a drunken slumber which brings no real refreshment to the sleeper.* As an ordeal, the lhiamba is supplied, after some preliminary ceremonies performed, both to accuser and accused in separate kinsus. They smoke simultaneously, and he who is the first to succumb to the power of the lhiamba is declared to be guilty either of the fault or of false witness. So far as the general subject of Lubuku is concerned, I will only now remark—since I intend treating the matter elsewhere—that the Bashilangé-Baluba are in reality without a religion. Some years ago, Calemba—who would amongst any people be a remarkable, and, indeed, in many respects a magnificent man—abolished Fetishism ; †—

---

* See Appendix II.

† Nevertheless throughout the Bashilangé country a curiously shaped obscene little idol, either female or fashioned like a priapus, and for the same reasons that the ancients placed that image in their fields and gardens, is still to be found at all cross-roads. It is generally about a foot in height, and stands on a round pedestal raised upon a pole a yard from the ground. In front a flat stone supports a basket, into which passing market-people, and all who have concluded a bargain, make a point of dropping grain or other

into its place Lubuku has crept.* Like all other African tribes with which I am acquainted, the Bashilangé believe in a future state, and possibly in the existence of One Supreme spiritual Being, but have otherwise few if any theological theories. They believe in witchcraft, necromancy, magic: with none of these beliefs does Lubuku interfere. Its initiatory rites are a profound and unfathomable mystery, and whether to describe Lubuku as a secret brotherhood, a religion, or a society for the propagation of licentiousness, I am uncertain. So far as the smoking of lhiamba itself is concerned, there can be no reasonable doubt but that the Matchioko introduced it primarily for purposes of fraud, since persons under the influence of that poisonous narcotic are temporarily insane, and therefore at the mercy of the first cruel and crafty trader that may come across them. But to return to our interview with Calemba. After preliminary greetings were over, and we had partaken of the luncheon we had brought with us, Lieut. Wissmann presented the various gifts that he had procured for the king, some of which were extremely handsome, and highly gratified the recipient. Having reported Congolemosch's submission, Lieut. Wissmann proceeded to open the all-important subject of his expedition across to the East Coast, and invited Calemba's assistance. The king replied that he could do nothing without the co-operation of his chiefs, nor could he himself leave or allow any considerable body of his people to leave home while

---

food, which any starving or destitute person is at liberty to eat; but no prayer or supplication whatever is offered before these fetishes, so far as I know. Would that in countries where, in like places, the Calvary stretches wide its "salutary arms to bless the waste" a similar truly charitable custom might obtain!

* See Appendix J.

the country was in an unsettled state, and especially while another powerful chief, Chilunga Meso, nominally his vassal, was in a state of hostility towards him. To this Lieut. Wissmann replied, that having anticipated this difficulty, he had sent for Chilunga Meso, and had arranged that he should be at Luluaburg on the following day: he begged that Calemba would meet him there. This the king discreetly refused to do, saying that he had nothing to propose to Chilunga Meso, though the latter had, or ought to have, something to propose to him; but he said that if Chilunga Meso liked to come to him after the palaver, he would be glad to see him, and to confer with him. He, moreover, promised to send his son to Luluaburg to meet Chilunga Meso and to conduct him thence to Kashia-Calemba. This brought our business to an end, and having inspected the house occupied some years previously by Dr. Poggé and Lieut. Wissmann, we took leave of Calemba and returned to Luluaburg.

BENI-NDUMBA.

CHAPTER VIII.

Chilunga Meso and his visions—The burning brandy—Senhor Caxavalla—His friendship with Chilunga Meso—Kasongo and the embassy from Ulungu—My return to Luebo—**General description of the route**—Dumba—Landslip—Beni-Muamba—Midnight alarm and Limo's bravery—Silence in the sunshine—Night in the forest—Awkward situation at Beni-Kashia—Arrival at Luebo.

NEXT day Chilunga Meso arrived. This most extraordinary man had obtained amongst his countrymen a reputation of a very peculiar nature. As a politician he was nothing. His entire want of interest in any terrestrial subject whatever makes it simply unaccountable that he should have troubled himself as to differences with Calemba: probably his circumstances were more potent to influence his conduct than were his inclinations. By fortune he was a powerful chief, by nature a prophet and a visionary. I made it my business to inquire most particularly into his sayings and doings, and I discovered that if he imposed upon others, he certainly imposed upon himself, and that whatever else he might be, he was scarcely what we understand by the term "clairvoyant." He was dreaded by the natives, partly because of his frequent violent fits and his extraordinary trances, but chiefly in consequence of his predictions, which, if the natives' testimony be good for anything, have all, or nearly all, been fulfilled, and in consequence also of his visions of, and communings with the departed. I can account upon physical grounds for his fits, his trances, and his visions, but to assign a cause for his accurate prediction of the future transcends my skill. Local occurrences, such as petty wars, epidemics, deaths, have been, it is said, foretold by him: in my own experience he predicted two most unlikely events, and his predictions were strictly verified: let those define the sources of his knowledge who know them; I do not. This strange chief was accompanied to Luluaburg by a dozen of his more presentable wives, and about 150 followers, fully armed. He brought with him a handsome present, and was no doubt prepared to make himself most agreeable: unhappily for such intentions, he was, if any man ever was, possessed of a devil. We received him in the dining pavilion, and he came in wearing an old shako, a Coldstream Guard's tunic, and a loin-cloth of native manufacture, his legs being entirely bare. As he was immensely tall (some 6 feet 5 inches), and much emaciated, his appearance would have been indescribably ludicrous had it not been for the expression of his face and wild steel-grey eyes.* After the customary greetings he seated himself, and began to converse, when a sudden rigor seemed to seize and stiffen his frame. He threw his arms wildly round, and continued to utter yelp after yelp—it is difficult to describe the cry. His spasms and outcries died away only to burst out with renewed frenzy, and he ended by foaming at the mouth in a fearful and disgusting manner. Three of his wives promptly held him down, or it is impossible to say what might have happened. In about ten minutes he recovered, and then astonished us all by talking most sensibly, showing himself a shrewd enough man, wise, and amenable to reason. After some argument and considerable persuasion, he undertook to submit to Calemba, and to make amends for any injuries that he had done or could be held to have done to the royal prerogative, but he took occasion at the same time to protest that he made these concessions solely on Lieut. Wissmann's account, and for peace' sake. For he maintained that although his relations with the world unseen unfitted him in great measure for wielding the regal power, yet, inasmuch as he was the recognised head of the ancient reigning dynasty of the Bashilangé, he had a better right to the throne than had Calemba, whose family was comparatively *parvenu*. The palaver concluded with the presentation of some handsome gifts to Chilunga Meso, who appeared altogether much pleased with his reception. As he had yielded to Calemba's request for an interview at Kashia-Calemba, he left us immediately for that place in company with the king's representative.

* Amongst the Bashilangé I have several times seen people with steel-grey eyes, which are, I believe, unknown in other African races.

I was greatly diverted by an incident occurring during these proceedings, which brought out more than one trait of the eccentric chief's character. Lieut. Wissmann, in order to astonish Chilunga Meso and his suite, filled a small glass with cognac, lighted it, and allowing it to blaze for a minute, blew out the flame and drank off the brandy. He then poured out a glass for his visitor, and having lighted it, handed it to him while burning. Fear, wonder, and curiosity were depicted on the faces of wives and attendants as they watched Chilunga Meso, who, seeing at once that he might venture to do what Lieut. Wissmann had already done, promptly extinguished the flame and drained the glass. Then looking round with an air of vast superiority, the chief thus addressed his people:—"Now, you see, I and the white chief are brothers; what he drinks I drink—we are one. But you—should any of you dare to touch this fetish drink, it will instantly destroy you, and I warn you, dream not of copying my courage. You well know that I am told your very thoughts, and should you even think of doing this—well, I will be much more than the death of any one of you."

The head-interpreter of Lieut. Wissmann's expedition, Senhor Manoel Caxavalla Silva da Costa, an Angolese gentleman of Dondo, whose acquaintance I had the pleasure to make during my visit to Luluaburg, had had some amusing, and indeed extraordinary, experiences with Chilunga Meso, which he was so good as to detail to me. I use the word "gentleman" advisedly in speaking of this estimable man, for such he was, and as such he was thoroughly respected by all who knew him, alike for his intelligence, his solid education, and vast knowledge of African languages, as well as for his sound sense, kindly humour, benevolence, and courtesy. When one thinks of the enormous influence lying in an interpreter's hands, the momentous issues which *may* hang upon the slightest turn given by him to a few brief sentences, the happiness, the welfare, the lives hourly affected by his skill and judgment, some estimate of the responsibilities of his office may be formed. It is high praise, therefore, to say that it would be impossible to imagine a man better fitted for the position than Senhor Caxavalla. From what he told me it appeared that Chilunga Meso had recognised in him— the man of many tongues—a spirit of divination kindred to his own, and he was accordingly instant in his requests that the interpreter would attend his *séances*, and assist at explaining his trance revelations and other communications from the spirits of departed friends. When their novelty had worn off, these proceedings became somewhat irksome to Senhor Caxavalla, and the distance of Chilunga Meso's place from Luluaburg, as well as the frequency of the *séances*, made the demands upon his time so serious that he was gravely fearing complications with Herr Bugslag unless he could contrive to curtail the number and duration of his absences from the station. When considering how this might be effected without offence, Senhor Caxavalla chanced to notice a lofty islet of rock rising out of the Lulua, where the river swirled and eddied towards some rapids in its course, and it occurred to him that could Chilunga Meso only be prevailed upon to betake himself to some such solitude, and there engage in imaginary intercourse with visionary beings, things in general would be a great deal better for many souls more mundane.* Accordingly he lost no time in representing to the seer that in the coming life the lot of that man would be lowly and his light obscure who had not here devoted time to solitary contemplation. This statement led to explanations, and of course the mention of the isolated rock, whither Senhor Caxavalla pretended that it had been his own practice periodically to retire. He alleged that it was as Bethel, a spot specially favoured by visits of immortals; and as Pisgah, a height from which visions of a promised country might be gained beyond the troubled flood of death. Chilunga Meso, much interested by this story, and anxious to participate in the visionary advantages set before him, begged to be taken to the islet, a desire which Senhor Caxavalla, as may be guessed, most readily promised to gratify, informing his neophyte, however, that his installation as hermit of the rock would have to be a solemn and carefully performed ceremony. To this end Senhor Caxavalla prepared "a cloak of religion" that would have done credit to a priest of Isis; a circular chasuble of the most ample mediæval proportions, manufactured from a partially worn-out cotton sheet. This he presented to the chief, together with a number of charms and sapheen, including a crucifix (of all things!), which were to be suspended round the neck. On the appointed day the seer and his instructor arrived just before sunrise at the islet in a canoe. Senhor Caxavalla, solidly standing at the water-level, produced a book of Roman Catholic devotions, from which, making a random selection, he gabbled over a multitude of Latin and Portuguese words and sentences,

---

* For the circumstance that probably suggested this idea to Senhor Caxavalla, see Appendix J.

the while Chilunga Meso, lean and scraggy, clothed in his cloak, and decorated with the mystic charms, mounted to the highest pinnacle of the rock. It is wonderful to me that the chief never suspected the impossibility of so hugely stout a man as the interpreter climbing in safety up and down so steep and slippery a place as the rocky islet, but certain it is that he did not, and that ever after Chilunga Meso would retire to its solitude, sometimes for days together, believing that his experiences were deeper and his spiritual vision more clear upon that favoured islet than in his home amidst the lives of other men.

Thinking of this particular companionship of beings so utterly dissimilar, a companionship produced neither by community of aims nor interests, still less by common participation in any of those deeper sympathies and soul-trying realities that make of mortals entirely opposite in outward nature an almost perfect unity, an immortal harmony, as of

> "Two notes of music,
> Made for each other though dissimilar,"

but by the force of circumstance alone, I am always reminded of Don Quixote and his servant Sancho Panza. The reference may not be quite complimentary to Senhor Caxavalla perhaps, but it is sufficiently just if we remember the maxim that an analogy must not be pressed.

When Chilunga Meso came to Luluaburg, he had in his company a number of Balungu, who, travelling under the leadership of a chief named Kasongo, had come on an embassy to Lieut. Wissmann, with the view of inducing him to promote the establishment of a station of the Free State in their country. They had journeyed from an immense distance, and through many and great perils, bringing with them a rich present of ivory, and a commendatory letter from Commander Cameron, who in his great journey "Across Africa" had passed through Ulungu, and being pleased with the behaviour of its inhabitants, had thus testified his satisfaction in writing. It was not possible for their wishes to be gratified, for their country, lying on the southern shores of Lake Tanganyika, although within the limits of the Free Trade area, is not only beyond the boundaries of the Congo State, but is separated from the nearest station by hundreds of miles of unexplored country, inhabited by savage and predatory races. The

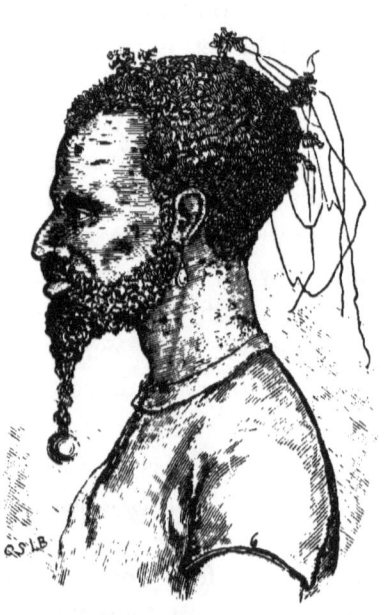

KASONGO—A PORTRAIT.

utmost, therefore, that Lieut. Wissmann could undertake was to visit Ulungu, and endeavour on the spot to ascertain what might be done towards bringing that country into communication with the civilising influences of the State—a promise he faithfully attempted to perform.

Amongst the native population in and around Luluaburg

a number of African tribes were represented besides those types of form, feature, and fashion to which one was more commonly accustomed. The Angolese soldiers (Ambakistas) looked very smart indeed in the red and white uniform of the German expedition, especially as contrasted with the sombre blue dress of our Luebo Zanzibaris; and there were Angolese women of the better class, some of whom were far from unattractive in appearance. The general bustle and life of the station, to say nothing of the agreeable companionship of the Europeans, made me regret the approach of the day on which I must bid farewell to my friends and return to my lonely life amongst the dark forests at Luebo.

My journey was by the same road as that by which we had come to Luluaburg, and as I was unfettered as to time, and without European companions, I had an excellent opportunity for making an exact survey of the route from the Miaw to the Luebo. The results of that survey may be summarised thus :— The whole district traversed lies within the basin of the Lulua, and upon the left bank of that river; all the streams crossed being its tributaries or their affluents. After leaving

SENHORA CAXAVALLA—A PORTRAIT.

the Miaw basin, which it crosses, the road ascends the Kalambaï valley, first crossing it. Thereafter a stream flowing independently to the Lulua is crossed, and the road again traverses a small portion of the upper drainage area of the Miaw, whence it ascends to a lofty tableland dividing the basin of that river from the Musisi valley, which it next gradually descends, and finally crosses. Leaving the Musisi, the road, making a considerable *détour*, crosses two small streams discharging themselves unitedly, or very near each other, into the Lulua, and finally enters the Luebo valley, which it gradually descends, until that stream is reached, where, at the station, it forms its junction with the Lulua. I was supposed to be carried in a hammock—for bullocks will not live at Luebo—but I was very little trouble to my bearers, as I generally preferred walking. The details of my survey and the incidents of my journey are as follows :—

From the Miaw the road, going N.W., crosses the narrow watershed dividing the basin of that tributary of the Lulua from its next neighbour, which, in default of a more exact name, I may call the Kalambaï stream. After leaving the Miaw, crossing a brook running into it, and going through open grass-land, the first small tributary of the Kalambaï is reached, at a distance of two miles from the Miaw. Another mile and a half of up and down grass-land brings us to the second affluent of the Kalambaï, which being crossed, we come two miles farther on to the main stream, at this point making a semicircular bend, flowing from N.E. to N.E., within which stands the town of Kalambaï.

We crossed the river, here, as elsewhere, flowing rapidly

over a gravelly and rocky bottom, between precipitous banks sparsely wooded, and reached the town, where we found food of all kinds abundant and cheap. This being a great place for onions (shalots), I procured two loads of them for planting at Luebo. Crossing the peninsula, one mile in breadth, on which the town stands, the road proceeds in north-half-easterly direction up the basin drained by the Kalambaï, though keeping mainly upon the higher ground. It crosses the stream again about four miles above the town, then turns N.N.W. for $2\frac{1}{2}$ miles, where it again crosses the stream, which here takes a sharp turn, forming a semicircle, half a mile being the chord of the diameter. Again crossing the river, the road turns due north for $2\frac{1}{2}$ miles, where thickly wooded swampy ground is reached, and the stream crossed for the last time.

From this point the road, now trending N.W., gradually ascends over fine prairie land for some ten miles, when Chinyama is reached, from which place the land slopes rapidly to the S.S.W. In this section of the road the watershed of the Kalambaï is crossed, and 200 yards beyond Chinyama town we come to the next affluent of the Lulua.

This is a deep and swift stream, running, at the point at which the road crosses it, in a north-north-easterly direction. The descent to the water is on both sides considerable, steep, and slightly wooded. For $2\frac{1}{2}$ miles west by half south from this river the ground gradually rises to Beni-Ndumba, $\frac{3}{4}$ mile beyond which place due west the road goes over a swamp for about 400 yards. Ndumba town is a poor place indeed, and rather a sad example of the state to which an unlimited use of lhiamba may bring a small community. Beyond the swamp the road, going N. by W., ascends a steep and barren hill, when the level of a grassy plateau is reached. From this plain fine views are obtained in every direction, and at about half its length (3½ miles) the road passes along a narrow neck between two great landslips, one on either side of the plateau: their depth might be 300 feet, and the fall quite precipitous. The direction of the landslip is towards N.E. and S.W. All this part of the country would, so far as I can see, answer magnificently for cattle-raising: there is neither tsetse nor the hurtful spear-grass so destructive to herbivorous animals. From the N.W. extremity of the plateau the road, descending slightly, turns for 4½ miles N. by E., when we come to a deserted town beside a stream: the former being surrounded, the latter fringed, with wood.

This stream runs towards the south-west, probably to the Miaw, into which drainage area we must thus have again descended on leaving the plateau. Leaving the river, the road goes W. by N. for 2½ miles, and thereafter due north for four miles, the ground rising rapidly until the level of another fine plateau is gained. Here we are crossing into the area drained by the Musisi, which rises presumably among a range of low hills running S.W. and N.E., visible across the wide depression forming the basin of that river. From this point the road turns in a north-westerly direction, gradually and continuously rising for 3¾ miles over grassy uplands until Beni-Muamba is reached. As the road approaches this town it skirts for some distance the edge of a vast landslip where the plateau has given way on its western side, falling into the lower grounds of the valley, a depth of not less than 400 feet. Up to this point my journey

had been entirely uneventful, but arriving at Beni-Muamba at 11.40 A.M. on the 21st, I found the place in great excitement owing to the recent ravages of some wild beast of unascertained species that was haunting the vicinity. Consequently my men could not sleep in the open, and other precautions had to be taken. In the afternoon I went down and sketched part of the nearest and most recent landslip—not a beautiful subject, indeed, however curious—and on returning to camp, I found the chief Mukanu anxious that I should see his wife, who, he said, was very sick. I found the poor woman suffering from inflammation of the lungs, and prescribed such simple treatment as the circumstances permitted. (She subsequently recovered, and showed a very grateful sense of the brief attention I had been able to give her.) During the night there was a terrible outcry, and on going out to inquire the cause, I was told that a lion (?) had just sprung into a hut where a number of people were sleeping and had seized a boy by the wrist, but that upon the others shouting out he had relinquished his prey and fled. I went immediately to the hut, and found that the poor lad's hand had been fearfully mangled. Luckily, as I had my case of instruments with me, and also a supply of caustic, I was able to dress and trim his wounds properly; otherwise, I am afraid the lad's life would have been sacrificed. On making a search, we found the footmarks of a very large beast, whether a huge leopard or a lion I cannot say. Thinking that the brute might possibly return, I took my rifle and waited about for him, but though during a vigil of some three hours' duration I heard several growls and similar noises from the long grass and neighbouring wood, I saw nothing of him. Limo, our caravan leader, an Angolese, volunteering to bear me company, remained by me for some time. Never could any man boast more of his valour and deeds of daring, or promise more bravely what great things he would do should the enemy present himself, when, suddenly, a loud harsh growl was borne to our ears, and poor Limo instantly collapsed: he rushed into his hut, and barricaded the door, which nothing could induce him to open until daylight dispersed his terrors, not much more than an hour before we resumed our journey at 7 A.M. on the 22nd.

Leaving this village, the road takes a north-north-west and a half northerly direction, and leads along the high grassy plains parallel with the Musisi (which is here flowing deep down in its densely wooded ravine some seven miles distant on our left), until $8\frac{3}{4}$ miles from Beni-Muamba, the Luisi is reached.

This small river, an affluent of the Musisi, flows swiftly from the east towards that river at the bottom of a deep and thickly wooded gorge, a descent of between 600 and 700 feet. Crossing this depression, and rising to about the same height, the road, holding a north-westerly course, passes a deserted town and plantations in the open grassy country (which is here somewhat diversified by belts of jungle of varying width), and arrives above the Musisi at a distance of twelve miles from the last stream crossed. The descent to the Musisi has been already described: all I have now to add is connected with my experience of the forest on its left bank as a camping-ground.

Having crossed the river, we camped for the night near to the treeless grassy uplands indeed, but well within the overarching wood, and at a height of several hundred feet above the water. In this region, save just at sunrise and before sunset, when nearly all the birds salute in noisy chorus the rising and the setting sun, the hours of daylight are the hours of silence. The sun, truly the most glorious emblem of omnipotence, makes the round tropic world his temple, and by his all-penetrating power compels to silence those that dwell within his presence; but when that presence is withdrawn, the animal creation wakes from its day-long constraint, and in a thousand ways tells forth its gladness and content. Thus, whether you camp within the forest or on the open plain, you have a ceaseless concert of strange sounds on through the hours of darkness, till the jungle-cock, fully two hours before the other birds awake, the earliest herald of approaching day, proclaims the silence that precedes the dawn. In crossing the river, I had observed that the spoor of buffalo and other game were deeply marked beside the ford, and determined, after camp was pitched and I had dined, to take my rifle, and ensconcing myself behind a sheltering bush, be ready for a shot, should any of the herd come by to drink. Accordingly, when night set in, the head-bearer going with me, I betook myself to the place of ambush. We clambered down through the thick tangle of the forest, where the long lianas of the dark-leaved india-rubber vines festooned the bright red cliffs; down through the thickets, where the delicate fresh green trails of creeping bamboo wreathed into almost impenetrable masses the creamy-flowered and jasmine-scented shrubs, all tints and colours blurred alike within the deepening gloom; down farther still into the darkness, where, above the trees that overarch the steep descent, the lovely lace-like orchilla weed spreads far her flowery veil; down almost to the murmuring river's edge, where, amid a clump of thorn-studded acacia, we had our ambush laid: a bush before us and a hastily constructed fence behind. When we began our watch, the myriad-voiced cicada and the croaking bull-frogs were in wildest chorus. Soon as the darkness deepened into night. the frequent hoot of owls was heard on all sides, followed by the plaintive whistle of the night-plover, the prolonged birr of the goat-sucker, so weird in its ventriloquial effect, and the booming of the bittern beside the stretches of still water underneath the fern-fringed hollowed banks. As we watched and waited for the buffalo, great bats came flitting overhead, the smart snapping of their teeth and their shrill mouse-like cries betraying what the noiseless movement of their wings concealed—their presence. Suddenly a wild scream strikes through the many voices of the night: it is repeated again and again as it comes nearer; —the cry of the fierce mbaku swinging himself from branch to branch in search of prey. And now, just overhead, once more that hideous shriek rings out triumphantly above the frantic chatter of a luckless colony of apes, for the mbaku is upon them, and their only safety lies in flight. At last, far off, we hear the buffalo, at first a distant lowing, and, as they near our ambush, now and then a crash, as the herd force their way through the thick undergrowth towards the water. But we wait and wait in vain: they are not coming to the ford, but are already going off by other brakes and openings farther up the stream. It would be worse than madness to attempt to follow in the dense and trackless wood, and so we seek our camp, climbing the steep rough path from out the darkness of the gorge. Just as we gain the safe circle of our fires, the rising moon breaks through the forest glades, and pours a silvery flood of light around us. Immediately the bull-frogs and the all-pervading chirrup of the crickets hush, while other sounds more distant reach our ears, borne from the prairie on the cool faint breeze: the answering cries of jackals, the hateful laugh of the cruel hyena, and now and then the mournful call of the spur-winged plover, silent in the dark.

Leaving the Musisi, the road almost reverses its direction, which, hitherto N.N.W., is now south-westerly, and proceeds for $7\frac{1}{2}$ miles through magnificent forest until a small stream is reached, which, like the Musisi and its affluent, flows at the bottom of a deep and wooded gorge. The direction of this stream is due north, and as it finds its way to the Lulua either independently or in conjunction with the stream next to be mentioned, this section of the road has thus brought us out of the area drained by the Musisi.

From this river the road turns for $1\frac{1}{4}$ miles W. by S., and then suddenly changes its direction to N.N.W., going across a high plain for $1\frac{1}{2}$ miles, at which distance another stream is reached, also deeply embosomed in a forest-covered ravine.

Crossing this river, the road next leads N. by W. half W. for $4\frac{3}{4}$ miles, of which distance $2\frac{1}{2}$ miles are dense forest. Thence inclining N.W. by W. for a distance of seven miles, the road brings us over grassy plains, from which towards the S.S.W. rise low hills more or less clothed with forest, into the basin of the Luebo. On our left we look down into the densely wooded valley, and skirting the

134   UNDER THE LONE STAR.

landslip which I had observed in my journey to Luluaburg, we come to Beni-Kashia. At this place I had now a
somewhat unpleasant duty to perform, which lack of time

LIANAS AT BENI-KASHIA.

alone had prevented our discharging previously. Considering its strategical importance, its pastoral advantages, and
its command of the land approach to Luebo, it would, in

any case, be highly desirable for the welfare of the station that Beni-Kashia should be in friendly hands; as long as the Luluaburg road, pursuing its present circuitous route, passes the village, an *entente cordiale* with its occupants is a necessity. Unhappily, the chief, Chikabo, was anything but a friend, except in word and outward show. As a matter of fact, he was a churl, and had been behaving with unprovoked hostility towards our people. He had in the first instance declined upon any terms to undertake the grazing of my goats and sheep, thereby causing us very great inconvenience; and when that question had been submitted to him, had seized the opportunity of my representative's presence to make certain disparaging remarks as to the order and government established at the station. Subsequently he refused to allow our messengers to and from Luluaburg to purchase food at his village, and had, in every possible way, done his utmost to nullify the civilising influences lately introduced into his neighbourhood. I had therefore to interview the chief upon this subject, and while our camp was being pitched, I gave him distinctly to understand that it was due to my reluctance alone to adopt extreme measures that his conduct had not been reported to Calemba, and I concluded by assuring him that if he did not at once change his policy he might expect very serious consequences indeed. I had not long returned to my camping-place when a thunderstorm that had been brewing all day burst suddenly right over our heads. The lightning struck a hut in the village, setting it on fire, and nearly killing a man who chanced to be within. On hearing of this, I went at once to the place where the poor fellow had been laid, and endeavoured to restore him to consciousness. As nothing of a fatal character is ever held in Africa to happen *ex ordine naturæ*, the catastrophe was instantly ascribed, and that as a matter of course, to my magic agency and skill. In my haste I had overlooked this contingency, or I should not have placed myself in the power of so vindictive and savage a gang as that by which I now found myself surrounded. I saw that the people were eyeing me with looks of anger and suspicion, and, without appearing to do so, I watched them arming themselves and stringing their bows. Perhaps it was for the best, but at the time I could not help most ardently wishing that I had not left all my arms in the tent, nor ventured thus alone into the village. Luckily the restoratives I had applied speedily availed to reanimate the injured man, and before the wretches had made up their minds to despatch me, or possibly before they were quite ready for the deed, I turned, and looking deliberately upon them, walked out of their village with as nonchalant an air as I could assume. More than one savage I saw fix his arrow to the bowstring, and as I strode back to my tent, leaving the scowling crowd behind me, I felt that any moment might bring my death-blow, and that the crisis of my life was come. Each second seemed an age, and when I regained the shelter of my tent. I had a momentary feeling as if years had gone since I left it. But it was no time for indulging thoughts or feelings; immediate action would, I knew, be requisite if an appeal to arms was to be avoided. Accordingly I sent Limo—he was less afraid, I fancy, of the Chiplumba than of lions—to inform Chikabo and his people that unless they should instantly disarm, and promise to behave with more amicability, I would call back the thunderstorm and utterly destroy them and their town. This preposterous message had the desired effect: we were

TÉVIVÉ (*Gossypium*).

suffered to remain unmolested during the night, and to continue our march at 7 A.M. on the 24th without further adventure of any kind.

Leaving Beni-Kashia, the road goes N.W. for 2¼ miles across the open plain. Then a belt of forest is reached, which the road, still going N.W., crosses for 1½ miles. Next a small grassy plain three-quarters of a mile broad is passed, after which we again come to the forest, and going through it N.W. by N. for two miles, we reach a small stream flowing W. to the Luebo, into which all the rivulets that are subsequently crossed between this and the station likewise drain.

At this point the road takes another direction. It now trends N.E. by N., crossing a small plain three-quarters of a mile broad, and thereafter a narrow belt of jungle rather less in width. Next going N.E. by E., we cross another plain 1½ miles broad, and then enter the dense and uninterrupted forest, through which the road gradually descends for 13¾ miles in a general direction of N.E. by E. half E., until we emerge once more into the dazzling sunlight and free air not far from the station at Luebo, of whose proximity the ceaseless boom of falling waters echoing for miles through the moist close woods has forewarned us.

"The Eastern hills of the Suebo."

BAKÈTÉ CHIEFS.

CHAPTER IX.

Senhor Carvalho's administration—The plantations and our crops—Misunderstanding with the Bakuba—Our Bakètè allies—Fireworks—Boat accident to Bakètè hunters on the Luebo—Ingratitude—Luebo Falls—Bakètè hunting-parties—Game of district—Slave-dealers.

LUEBO was altogether much as we had left it. I found more work accomplished in the way of clearing and preparing for our plantations than I had anticipated. Everything else was in excellent order, and I felt that I had abundant cause to be grateful to Senhor Carvalho for his painstaking management during my absence. Before leaving for Luluaburg I had assigned to him a plot of ground whereon to build huts for his workmen and a store for himself. I was now glad to find that, for all practical purposes, the worthy man—whom I had learnt entirely to dissociate from his partner—was likely to be a fixture at our station. His history and circumstances appealed in many ways to my sympathies, while he, for his part, was not unsympathetic with us: he was thoroughly our well-wisher, and he was fitted by long intercourse with the natives, and his own bitter experiences of the hard dealings of traders, to be a trustworthy adviser in many a difficulty. Yet in respect of one matter, occurring soon after my return, I always thought that had Carvalho chosen to enlighten me as to his dealings with our Bakuba neighbours during my absence, an unfortunate misunderstanding that threatened at one period to originate a very considerable trouble might have been avoided. But before I go fully into that story I must turn to what was engrossing my almost undivided attention at this time—I mean the plantations.

Unless we were to continue for another season to be dependent upon our native neighbours for such supplies as the precarious steam communication with Léopoldville did not furnish, our clearings must be finished, the ground tilled, and the crops sown before the rains should set in.[*] The method we pursued was to clear away the jungle undergrowth and the upper branches of the larger trees with axes, and then, having selected and removed all those straight pieces which promised to be useful for carpentry and building purposes, we piled the smaller boughs together in heaps round the trunks we wished to get rid of without the labour of felling them, and set fire to the whole. The roots were next carefully stubbed up and burnt, all the ashes being evenly spread over the ground, with which

---

[*] Some few statistics calculated to give an idea of the difference between the seasons at Luebo will be found in the Appendix K.

THE PLANTATIONS AT LUEBO. 141

they were incorporated by a thorough hoeing. We then fenced in the land, and parcelled it out according to the nature and requirements of the crops we intended to

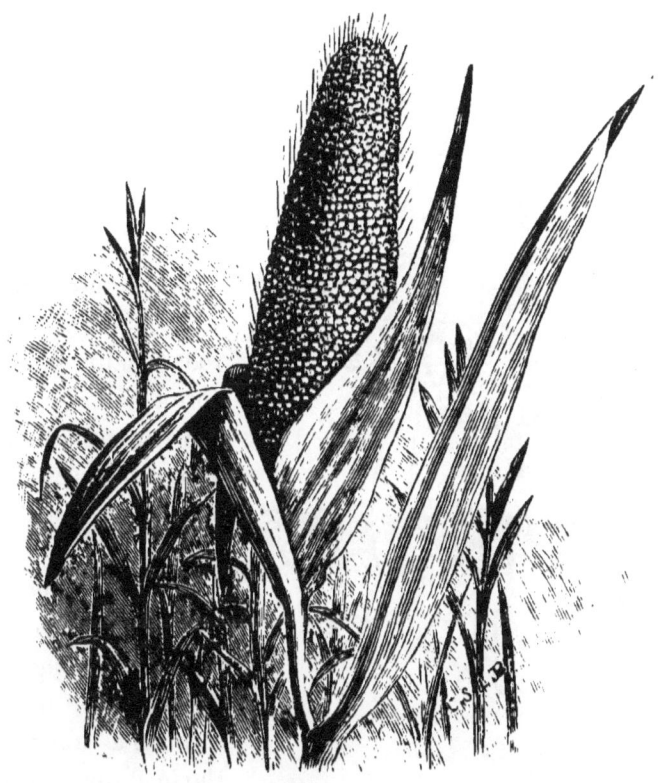

MFOSHÉ (*Sorghum*).

grow. Eventually deep drains made of broken stone were put in, but not until after we had reaped our first harvest. Some ten acres of the lowest ground next the river were sown with Indian-corn, slips of manioc six feet apart being put in at the same time, and a crop of yams was also set in this part of the plantations. Another ten acres at a higher level was planted with mtama (*Holcus sorghum*) and hill-rice. Besides these principal crops we grew a number of vegetables and esculents, many of them for my own especial use: onions, cabbage, okras, tomatos, gourds, turnips, lettuce, endive, celery (a complete failure), beans, some pot-herbs, beetroot (a failure), a little cotton and sugar-cane. I planted also an abundance of pineapples and grenadilhas, and some fruit trees, of which more anon. I had made a large clearing in the jungle at a considerable distance from the station, on the road towards Beni-Kashia, where I established the burial-ground, and also a plantation of ground-nuts ("mpinda") some fifteen acres in extent.

MPINDÉ NGUBA (*Arachis*).

I may now give the narrative of the misunderstanding referred to above. Senhor Carvalho complained to me on

A DISQUIETING RUMOUR.

my return that the Bakuba farther down the river had become hostile, that they had been vowing all manner of vengeance against us, and he attributed an importance to their threats which seemed to me quite unmerited,—an opinion which his persistence in denying that he had had any quarrel with them tended to confirm. Of the nature of the Bakuba's feelings towards us I was not, however, kept long in doubt. Lieut. Wissmann having given me instructions to make a thorough survey of the Lulua from the Luebo to the Kasaï, I took an early opportunity of going down the stream for the purpose of beginning this business from near the Luebo end. Senhor Carvalho was to bear me company, but on embarking he was so urgent that I should take arms for the rowers, that, since I saw no reason for such a proceeding, I suggested his remaining behind. This, however, he refused to do, and as I compromised matters by taking my own three rifles and an ample supply of ammunition, his courage so far revived as to enable him to profess his belief in the absence of real danger, a belief which I now think I myself should not have shared had I only known as much as he could have told me. Having gone some little distance and well out of view of the Luebo mouth, we drew near a landing-place on the right bank, where we saw a crowd of Bakètè beckoning us to approach. We immediately steered to them, and learning that some of these people were bearing fish and palm-wine to the station for barter, we relieved them of their loads without further trouble to themselves, for, when practicable, I always carried with me a stock of the small change of the country, viz., beads, cowries, and brass rods. The Bakètè then inquired whether

I intended going farther down-stream, and on hearing that I did, endeavoured to dissuade me, alleging that the Bakuba were greatly exasperated, and were preparing to attack us should they obtain any chance of doing so successfully. As I deemed this to be mere idle gossip, I continued our course down the river to the point at which I had determined to begin the survey. We had not gone far from the Bakété, and were still keeping to the same bank, when we saw a Bakuba chief sitting just outside a fishing-hut, who no sooner saw us than he gathered up his bow and arrows and made off into the jungle. Wondering what this unwonted conduct might portend, I ran the boat on the beach and jumped out, but the only people I could see were two men on a large partly wooded island about ninety yards from the shore. Thither I proposed we should immediately go, both to demonstrate our friendliness, and to ascertain the true state of the Bakuba disposition towards us : the excuse for our approach being the purchase of fish. As we neared the island the men raised shouts and cries, which were speedily echoed from the jungle, whence almost immediately a number of fully armed men sprang out. I stood up in the boat, brandishing beads and brass rods, calling out that we wanted to trade. The only answer was a flight of arrows, by which one of our poor fellows in the bows was severely wounded. We replied as rapidly as we could with our rifles, and four of the enemy went down, their comrades taking to flight. I thereupon deliberately began my surveying operations, tacking from side to side of the river for the sounding as occasion required. Probably onlookers in the wood believed we were occupied in setting some irresistible fetish, destined to ruin the fisheries or destroy their arms. On returning to the station, we found every one in a wild state of excitement. A report (which had lost nothing in the telling) of what had occurred having long preceded us, the Niapara had placed the Zanzibaris under arms, and was busy with preparations for defence when we arrived. Several Bakètè chiefs also were anxiously awaiting our return, being extremely desirous, on their own account, to prevent any further hostilities between their formidable neighbours. After a time more Bakètè arrived, and earnestly implored me to send messengers to the dreaded Bakuba, to acknowledge that we had trespassed in going down the river without their permission, and to offer compensation for having fired upon them at the island. To such preposterous demands only one reply could be given. Telling the Bakètè that they must choose whom they would befriend, I assured them that if they elected thenceforth to serve the Bakuba, and help them against me, I had no objection to fight their united forces; but if, on the other hand, they desired to be free from an ancient thraldom, and to cast in their lot with us, I was willing to undertake their defence against the Bakuba, as I had previously done against the Batua Bankonko.* This assurance ended their doubtful attitude, and they agreed to help me in defending the station should occasion render such defence necessary. We passed a somewhat restless night, our fortifications being incomplete, but next day (July 5th) our Bakètè allies mustered in great force, about a thousand camping near Kassèngè, on the other

---

* Whom I had forcibly expelled in March 1886 from two of the small villages near Kassèngè, of which they had possessed themselves.

side of the Lulua. In the course of the day the Bakuba advanced to the attack, but seeing the odds ranged against them, they refrained from making any demonstration until late in the afternoon, when their war-canoes, on rounding the point below the station, came within range of our howitzer, and their hopes of success were speedily annihilated. When night closed in, I had a grand pyrotechnic display, as we were so fortunate as to possess a large quantity of fireworks amongst our stores. The coloured lights especially caused some curious and beautiful effects, and a couple of war-rockets, that went screaming and hissing over the river and through the trees, drawing for so great a distance a trail of light behind them, caused the utmost terror and consternation alike to friends and foes. Next morning, in answer to a general invitation given through our Bakètè mediators, two Bakuba chiefs ventured to the station. One, whom I recognised as the chief of the men who had fired upon us on the 4th at the island, I singled out for reproach; to the other I showed such complaisance as I thought fitting, and made him a small present. I gave them distinctly to understand that if they had any complaints against our people, they need not fear to come to me and make them known, for I would redress all grievances, but that causeless hostility to the station people would not only be resented by us, but very severely and surely punished. It is worthy of note that I was never able to ascertain the precise nature of the offence that had been given to the Bakuba; but whatever it may have been, the storm had the effect of clearing the atmosphere, for we had no subsequent misunderstandings—in fact, we continued excellent neighbours during the remainder of my residence at Luebo.

This war-scare quickened our movements as to the completion of our defences. The ramping along the river fronts, and the palisading on the land side, were soon finished. Here we made a regular fosse, 18 feet broad at the top, and 14 feet at the bottom, the depth being about 8 feet. The approach from the land was over a gorge, flanked by a loop-holed house, and the entrance through the palisade was secured with bars. Other progress had been made, and my own house was finished soon after the fortifications, but the bath-house and some minor offices were not completed until a later date. We had begun road-making also in the only direction in which road-making could be undertaken, viz., towards Lulnaburg. The old native path meandered through the limits of the new roadway, which is perfectly straight, an even and gradual ascent at about one in twenty-five from the station to the burial-ground, a distance of some 1200 yards. The road lay between the plantations and the thick forest, and was planted on both sides in its lower portion with plantains and bananas, chiefly the former, as for some unknown reason they succeed better in this district than bananas. I set other fruit-trees also, such as are to be met with in the native plantations, but I cannot, of course, say how they succeeded.

For some weeks after the unpleasantness with the Bakuba nothing of importance occurred to vary the monotony of our administrative routine. The plantations and the building operations were close at hand, and their supervision took me no distance from my own door. The survey of the river afforded some change, as long as it lasted, and an occasional day of hunting was quite a pleasing excitement. Once or twice I went with the Bakèté hunters, who used frequently to come across to our side of the river in pursuit of game. They were always careful to ask my permission, and were most generous to me in their subse-

BAKÈTÉ HUNTERS.

quent distribution of the spoil. The Luebo jungles were favourite hunting-grounds of the Bakèté, and thus, and in looking out for timber trees, I got to know a good deal of that quarter of our neighbourhood. One day I came upon some fine grassy plains not above a mile from the station, but upon the other side of the Luebo, and at a considerable elevation. Being much impressed with the capabilities of this position as a site for dwellings and plantations, I made a regular survey of it, and marked out five allotments. The comparatively high altitude of this locality, the absence of swamp in the quarters from which prevailing winds blow, the sandy soil, and ample outfall, all combine to recommend it as a sanatorium for the neighbouring station, which cannot, I fear, prove a healthy residence for either natives or Europeans, at least for any long or continuous period. Without making a regular survey of the Luebo, I contrived in the course of several brief excursions to become acquainted with the main features of that river in its lower portion, and for some considerable distance above the falls. Here and there stretches of navigable water are to be met with, but the interruptions are so numerous that no use is ever made of the upper stream as a means of communication, save in the event of the Bakètè and other hunters launching a canoe occasionally on the still water reaches in order the better to pursue their quarry. In consequence of this practice an accident occurred, which only by a miracle escaped a tragic ending. Some half-dozen hunters one day came into the station from Kassèngè, asking me to lend them a light canoe in order to launch it above the first falls, their own canoe being inconveniently heavy for the porterage. On inquiry, I found they were in quest of large bats, which during the daytime may be seen depending from the branches of trees overhanging the river. As I refused to lend our canoe, the huntsmen were obliged to take their own. Some two hours after they had gone I chanced to be out on the Luebo side of the station, when, to my horror, I saw fragments of the canoe borne past me by the rapid current. Fearing that a really dreadful disaster had happened, I hurriedly sent out some men with orders to search for the hunting-party at and beyond the falls. They returned more speedily than I had anticipated, bringing with them one of the hunters, in a half-drowned condition, whom they had found in the river clinging to the branch of a tree. This man reported that, in the excitement of securing the bats, they had somehow lost their paddles, and shoving off from the trees beneath which they were before their loss was known, the canoe had been caught by the swift eddy, and was hurried over the rapids immediately above the falls. It was instantly upset, and the men, none of whom could swim, were engulfed in the rushing torrent. What had become of them he knew not, and indeed was quite unable to give any account as to how he himself had contrived to reach the branch whence my people rescued him. However, we had no sooner given the others up for drowned than, to our utter amazement, they one and all came in, more or less exhausted, and bedraggled indeed, but safe and sound, having in various ways succeeded in reaching the bank. I administered such restoratives as seemed requisite, and had them ferried across the Lulua, remarking that they ought to be grateful to a kind Providence for their truly wonderful escape. Will it be believed that any human beings could be so utterly sceptical of the simplest laws of nature, so absurdly blind to the most evident connection between cause and effect? These hardened and ungrateful blockheads could see nothing wonderful in their unaccountable deliverance from the jaws of instant death, but only in the fact of their coming into any kind of misadventure at all—a circumstance which they

FALLS OF THE LUEBO.

positively ascribed to my black magic, and not to their own foolhardiness! This truly African disbelief in physical law is doubtless inseparable from a low position in the scale of human knowledge, and we laugh at it:—Are we to consider a corresponding belief in Divine interference with the laws of nature as equally ridiculous, or as indicative of a complete and perfect knowledge of the universe?

THE WESTERN FALLS OF THE LUEBO.

The falls of the Luebo, thus frequently referred to, occur in the course of that river about a mile above its junction with the Lulua, and at a point where the stream is divided into two nearly equal portions by an island measuring somewhat under a mile in length. The waters in the eastern channel are broken into several separate cascades, that farthest down the stream having a fall of over 18 feet, and being by far the most imposing in appearance. The western channel, on the other hand, is, with the exception of a considerable step at its base, a continuous boiling rapid, unbroken in its course by any marked variation in the angle of its descent. The total difference in the level of the river-bed from top to bottom must be considerably over one hundred feet. The surrounding forest is dense on all sides, and though it enhances the general beauty of the prospect, its rank luxuriance in places greatly intercepts the view of the water, and, in union with the extremely tortuous character of the river's course, mars, to some extext, what would otherwise be an unusually fine piece of water-scenery.

The Bakètè hunting-parties that ranged these forests and the adjoining plains were generally large companies, consisting of as many—sometimes—as two hundred members, and about half that number of dogs, the latter being provided with wooden bells strapped under their bellies. Each man is armed with a bow, a number of arrows, a spear, and a knife. Most of them carry nets. The principle on which the Bakètè manage their hunting is identical with that practised in India by the Government elephant-hunters under the name of "Keddah." The plan of the chase may be said to consist of a vast triangle, of which the base, and sides in the direction of the base, are of indeterminate length, but having the apex cut off by a circle described from a centre without the triangle, the said circle, and adjacent portions of the sides, being formed of nets stretched upon stakes. The base of the triangle is, of course, the jungle district which it is intended should be beaten for game. When the Bakètè huntsmen have observed the recent spoor of any kind of smaller game and antelopes, they enclose with their hunting-nets and stakes a suitable piece of bush-ground for the "hot corner" as described. The company then disperse, keeping at as regular intervals from each other as possible, and thus going round the outside of the area which they design to drive, they enclose a considerable tract of country, sometimes miles in extent. Then, as the hunters gradually converge, the game, frightened by the approaching and increasing noise of men and dogs, charge along towards the only point in which silence seems to promise safety. The hunted creatures, thus nearing the vortex, are guided in their flight by the enclosing wings or netted sides of the triangle into the fatal corner, whence few indeed escape alive from the spears and arrows of the huntsmen, who are already there before them. Sometimes, however, a buffalo or other large animal will be enclosed within the nets, when not unfrequently the conditions of the chase are reversed, and the hunters become the quarry. On one of those occasions on which I was present a large buffalo—than which, in my opinion, no animal in Africa is more dangerous to be hunted—destroyed some of the nets, and gored one poor fellow so frightfully that he died almost instantaneously.

As I have before intimated, the game preferred by the Bakètè are the smaller animals to be found, I cannot say abundantly, for game is not abundant, if indeed we except bats, rats, and other vermin, in their part of the country. In this region much of the larger game common enough in East Central Africa simply does not exist—zebras, giraffes, rhinoceros being unknown. There is, however, one animal belonging to the catalogue of large game which I believe to be a speciality of this country—an extremely fine antelope, called by the natives Bambangala. I have not met with it elsewhere in Africa, nor seen it figured or described by others. In size it is as large as a mule, of a bright chestnut colour, striped with creamy-white, much in the manner of a zebra, on the back and sides, and dappled on the neck and flanks. The belly is white, as is also the scut. The horns are not in

BAMBANGALA.

any way remarkable either for size or form. Besides buffaloes, which are numerous only in the grassy tracts of the Bashilangé country, I have observed leopards, panthers, civets, hyenas, the snow-leopard, numerous species of wild cats, otters, onças, the Cape hunting-dog, jackals, the sloth-like creature called "mbaku," and, very rarely, the lion. Elephants abound in the forests about the Luebo, and there are hippopotami in all the rivers. There are quantities of ichneumon, the mention of which little creature reminds me of the unfortunate abundance of alligators, which, however, cannot possibly be accounted as game. Amongst the creatures hunted by the Bakètè for food are, occasionally, the eland (though it is rather large game for them to tackle, and is rarely met with), the water-buck, the smaller kudu, the red bush-buck, the water or reed buck, and the saddle-back or harnessed antelope, so called from the curious white markings on back and sides; the bush-pig, the porcupine, the earth-pig, the large jungle-rat, a kind of squirrel, an ant-bear, the sibissi (a species of hare), and monkeys of every description. They also trap and eat a large field-rat, the ordinary field-mouse, and bats. The common house-rat they do not eat, and being much plagued by their depredations, they highly appreciated the achievements of a domestic cat that I had imported. Other creatures that they take for food are the iguana and several kinds of lizards; the land-tortoise (the water-tortoise and fish of all kinds being generally obtained from the Bakuba or Baluba fishermen); snakes, including the boa constrictor; grubs and caterpillars; the larvæ of the white ant, and also, at one stage of its existence, the white ant itself, and locusts, but these last-named are happily rare. Of birds, they take, by means of nets and traps, as well as by shooting with arrows, pigeons both green and grey, guinea-fowls, giant plantain-eaters, toucans, parrots, quails, water-hens, a kind of partridge, and occasionally wild ducks and Egyptian geese, the various waders, ibis, and eagles when they can get them. Altogether I am afraid that, although the list is a long one, the fare it indicates is but meagre;

156   UNDER THE LONE STAR.

and although civilisation when introduced may greatly lessen the natural food resources of the country, one of its chiefest blessings will be the supply of nourishing and thoroughly wholesome sustenance to the inhabitants.

ANT-BEAR AND ANT-HILL.

Towards the end of August it was reported to me that there had arrived in our vicinity, from the country to the east, a caravan of slave-dealers known as Bihanos These people, inhabitants of Bihé in Angola, have been long wont to travel into the interior for the purpose of exchanging salt and other articles of barter for such slaves as they could obtain by means so far fair, or those means failing, by kidnapping the unfortunate victims of their cupidity. Thereafter, in returning to their own country, where their living merchandise has become valueless, or almost so, since Portugal has made serious profession of suppressing the slave-trade, they generally make, for obvious reasons, a considerable *détour* into some suitable region, and there exchange their slaves for ivory, which can, of course, be easily negotiated in Bihé. It was thus that the Bihanos referred to had come into the Bashilangé country, and they had made a good many bargains before I was aware of their presence. Commander Cameron has so fully exposed the inhumanity of these people, as he witnessed it just at the end of their palmier days, that I need say nothing about them beyond noting the fact that I took immediate measures to secure their expulsion from my district, and it was satisfactory to find that my orders were promptly obeyed; within three days not one member of the caravan remained in our neighbourhood.

GROUND-NUT OIL-MAKING.

CHAPTER X.

Visit to Lukenga Manena—My namesake—Dishonesty of João Domingos—Expedition against Biombé—Temporary imprisonment of the chief—Ground-nut oil—Carvalho's boat-building and project—Arrival of the *Stanley* with my successor—The Sanford expedition—I leave Luebo—Accident to the *Stanley*—Sacred island of Kimeh—Kwamouth and the Catholic Mission—The Abbé Krafft—Kinchasa and Léopoldville once more.

SHORTLY after the Bihanos incident I made an excursion up the country on the right bank of the Lulua, and proceeded farther up the river than Luluaburg, though of course in a different direction. My object was to visit Lukenga Manena,

a powerful and remarkably well-disposed Bashilangé chief, who had repeatedly pressed me to do so, and had been at some pains to conciliate my good opinion. The road lay through Kassèngé and the Bakété country, passing through fine undulating grass-lands, forest, and jungle, but intercepted by no deep ravines or uninhabited districts. On the contrary, our eyes were constantly gladdened by large and beautifully kept plantations, many neat and populous towns, and a happy and industrious people. Only four streams worthy the name of rivers had to be crossed, and the descent in each case was easy and gradual. On my way I saw Congolemosch, but not Chilunga Meso, who was away from home; whether having betaken himself to his hermitage or not I forget, but my impression is that he had gone to visit Calemba. Nothing occurred which could be esteemed of special interest, at least of a kind different from that which I have described as having happened elsewhere. I regret much that I did not take any observations or make a route chart, but, as a matter of fact, the damp heat of Luebo had told upon me a good deal, and I was disinclined to uncalled-for exertion of any kind when out, as I was, for a little holiday. In the course of my journey I stopped to visit a namesake of mine, a chief called Chienvu. I say "namesake" because, when first I came into the Bashilangé country, the people, believing in metempsychosis, had named me "Chienvu," deeming me to be the embodiment of a chief of that name who had died some years previously. In this I only shared an honour done to Lieut. Wissmann and Dr. Wolf, who, in like manner, received from the natives appellations denoting their identity with departed chiefs. I had left the station once more in Senhor Carvalho's hands, and found everything in excellent order on my return. Our crops in the new plantations were a success: the sorghum, a fine heavy crop, being by this time reaped and in store: the rice having been sown so as to ripen in relays, only a small quantity was harvested, but it was excellent. I was thus enabled to begin the draining in the plantations and elsewhere. The drains were square built, of rough stone, a quantity of small or broken stones being superimposed between the roof of the drain and the soil.

Immediately after my return from visiting Lukenga Manena a circumstance occurred, which, although perhaps trivial in itself, serves to illustrate some of our administrative difficulties. We had in our service at Luebo an Angolese, by name Jaõ Domingos, a pure-bred negro, but acquainted with the Portuguese language, able to read and write, and withal, nominally, a Christian. I naturally felt that a man of this kind could be more or less trusted, and accordingly, despite a word of warning from Dr. Wolf, I detached him for service on the Bakètè side of the river. There I had placed him as guard of the flock of goats belonging to the station, which, in consequence of our failure to obtain pasturage for them from Chikabo of Beni-Kashia, were kept on the other side of the Lulua, pursuant to an agreement for their grazing concluded with the Bakètè chiefs. I had been home a day or two—a fact of which, as it afterwards appeared, Jaõ was ignorant—when a couple of miserable goats were received at the station to be entered on the books and branded; which being done, I forthwith forgot all about the occurrence. Not long after I was perplexed by the arrival of a messenger from a Bashilangé-Baluba chief, Debinga Debeha, who resided across the Lulua some six days' march eastward from Luebo, requesting the gift of a gun. As I had never received a visit from this chief nor come into contact with him in any way, I considered the request unreasonable, and said as much, adding that not only were we unacquainted, but that as Debinga Debeha had never sent me a present, I did not see why I should send one to him. To my surprise the messenger, a young man, who was, by-the-bye, the chief's son, replied that I was surely mistaken, for that his father had only recently sent me a present consisting of two slave-boys, but that his messengers had been told that I would not see them, the present being quite inadequate, and that they must bring in addition a bullock, a girl and a boy. Further conversation and reflection decided me to give the gun, with which the young man departed, promising to return as speedily as possible with the fullest proofs of the truth of his allegation. In the meantime, although nothing had transpired which directly implicated Jaõ, yet my suspicions and the whole circumstances surrounding the transaction pointed him out as the culprit, and I therefore lost no time in sending for him. Being interrogated, Jaõ at once admitted having encountered Debinga Debeha's messengers, and having received the present—two goats; but he asserted that believing me to be away from home, he had relieved the messengers of their charge, and dismissing them, had sent the goats over to the station to be duly entered in the books—a circumstance, he remarked, that must surely be within my knowledge and recollection. He acknowledged receiving the two lads, and volunteered the statement that he had also sold them for his own profit, but he maintained that they were sent to him by Debinga Debcha in payment of a debt due by that chief, and that they had nothing to do with the present sent for me, which consisted solely of the two goats. Kabèmbé, the chief of the village where Jaõ and the goats were located, and who accompanied him on this occasion, confirming all his statements, my perplexity was increased. However, I told Jaõ that, by his own confession, he had been guilty of a most serious breach of the law in trading in slaves, who, had they come into my hands, would have been immediately emancipated, but that, as he did not appear to have acted from any evil intention, I would this once overlook his misconduct, provided that he would redeem the two unfortunates. This did not satisfy Jaõ; he would have no complicity with crime; his probity had been impugned, and he preferred quitting the station; and concluded his protestations by requesting that he might be removed to Luluaburg, where he had a brother in the service of Lieut. Wissmann's expedition, from whom he could obtain the means to repurchase the two slaves, as I demanded that he should. Duly impressed by this edifying exhibition of injured honesty and refined feeling, I hastily granted his request, giving him a transfer note for his pay, four days' rations and ammunition for the journey, and I allowed him to take his rifle. Some two days after Jaõ's departure, Debinga Debcha's son returned with his witnesses, and I had to send for Kabèmbé. To my amazement, this worthy, on being confronted with the witnesses, reluctantly confessed his cognisance of Jaõ's fraud, which had, he admitted, consisted not only in misrepresenting my disposition towards Debinga Debeha, and demanding a larger present, as the witnesses had alleged, but in appropriating the two lads, and then representing part of the price he had received for them, viz., the two goats, as the present Debinga Debeha had sent to me. Moreover, the story of that chief's indebtedness to Jaõ turned out to be a pure fabrication. Thus enlightened, I sent forthwith to M. de Mácàr, requesting him to arrest Jaõ should he arrive at Luluaburg, and to send him to me. At the same time I sent expresses to all the chiefs in those directions whither Jaõ was likely to turn in order to effect an escape from the country, commanding them to stop the man and bring him uninjured to Luebo. In consequence of these measures, Jaõ was soon brought into the station, very much against his will indeed, but securely. He had, of course, never attempted to go near Luluaburg, but only to escape to Angola. Other accusations were brought forward, and he was tried and convicted of slave-dealing and breach of trust, being finally taken down to the coast, there to undergo two years' hard labour on board the hulk.

The next event that I have to chronicle in the history of my work at Luebo necessitates a reference to the period of our misunderstanding with the Bakuba, or rather to the week preceding that trying and critical occasion. Not many days after my return from Luluaburg I received a despatch, dated 26th June 1886, which had followed me from that station. It was accompanied by a letter from M. Le Marinel, and the purport of both communications was that I was to prepare and hold myself in readiness to co-operate at an early date in a military demonstration against the people at Biombé, the Chiplumba-Bashilangé town, or rather towns, situated between the Kasaï and Lulua rivers, some three hours' march from Luebo. The chief of that place, Kalonda, a cousin of the churlish Chikabo at Beni-Kashia, was imbued with similar feelings towards the State, and the root of bitterness was in both cases one and the same, viz., the intrigues of the Matchioko. These mischief-workers, finding us a hindrance to their own traffic, or suspecting that we should soon become one, lost no time in representing to the Chiplumba that the authorities of the Congo State came into the country for the one purpose of imposing taxes and oppressing the aborigines. This poison, which at Beni-Kashia had produced the immediate result of that hostility towards ourselves which I have already mentioned, developed at Biombé, removed by its situation from all friction with *us*, a spirit of rebellion against Calemba. The whole subject had been under discussion when I was at Luluaburg, and it was then determined that I should remonstrate with Chikabo, as already detailed, and that Kalonda should be left to more forcible treatment by Calemba. From the despatch of the 26th of June it now appeared, however, that Kalonda was to be brought to reason by a force from Luluaburg under M. Le Marinel, and that Luebo was to form the basis of operations. The news I received from Luluaburg, I may here remark, was to the effect that on the following day Lieut. Wissmann was to set out for Ulungu in company with Kasongo and his party. As things turned out, the demonstration against Biombé never came off; the prolonged absence of Lieut. Wissmann and other deterrent causes delayed the business at Luluaburg, while at Biombé and Luebo the mere lapse of time and practical experience of our pacific conduct conciliated the native good-will, and gradually produced a better state of feeling both towards Calemba and the State. About the middle of the Bakèté harvest, however—in September—circumstances rendered necessary the adoption of active and stringent measures. Food getting scarce, and there being many to feed, I had sent parties far afield to procure grain and other provisions at as reasonable rates as might be met with. Finding that Biombé was the cheapest market and best supplied in the country at the time, my people went thither and returned more than once, making bargains to the satisfaction of all parties. This was precisely what the Matchioko did not desire. They renewed their calumnies against us, and on receiving the reply that while experience had shown us to be inoffensive in conduct, and altogether unlike what had been pictured, yet it was equally clear that we were formidable neighbours, and that it was therefore unadvisable to disoblige us, the Matchioko rejoined with clamour, insisting that the Bakwa Biombé must decide between friendship with them or with us. Accordingly, valuing above all things the skill of the Matchioko as blacksmiths, the Bakwa Biombé elected to retain their services at the expense of their own trading relations with us, and when next my people came to market, they were insulted, fired upon, and driven off. This being reported to me, I took steps for bringing our neighbours to reason. In the first place, having acquainted Calemba with this occurrence, I sent messengers to inquire the ground of such behaviour, and demand that the former friendly intercourse should be restored. These messengers were insulted and dismissed without any reply being given to my message, and all further attempts to open communications having failed, I determined to give the Bakwa Biombé a salutary lesson. The operation I proposed undertaking was of the nature of a surprise, with the object of capturing the chief, and detaining him a prisoner until he and his people should give security for better behaviour: it was, of course, in the highest degree desirable to avoid all destruction of life or property, and instructions were issued accordingly. I made a plan of the line of march, and the positions to be occupied, and divided the attacking force into two companies, the larger of which, under the command of Bimba, our interpreter, and Mohamadi, the Zanzibari niapara, I despatched at nightfall. They were to reach the vicinity of Biombé as speedily as possible, halting there some hours for rest, and were finally to take up a position close to the towns about 3 A.M. I myself went down the river later with the smaller force, landing at two o'clock, and proceeded through the dense forest along the beaten track towards the towns. I was careful to send out feelers in advance along either flank, but we arrived at our destination without misadventure of any kind. We had, of course, brought rockets with us, and on coming within a short distance of the stockade fired one — the appointed signal — which had scarcely burst when our co-operating party fired a volley, and we all advanced to enter the town. The Bakwa Biombé were not wholly taken by surprise, and they resisted a short time, so that we had seven men wounded. However, we succeeded in our object without much further difficulty, capturing Kalonda and taking him away a prisoner. We marched back to the landing-place, leaving the towns and plantations uninjured, the land party returning by the river's bank and keeping parallel with us. The Bakwa Biombé were greatly alarmed by this prompt manifestation of our power, and fled temporarily from their towns. After a few days, when their return and submission had been reported to me, I restored Kalonda under certain conditions and promises, and I believe that he was more impressed by the mildness of the restraint imposed upon him during his brief captivity than by the promptitude with which he had been arrested.

The last agricultural, or quasi-agricultural, operation over which I presided at Luebo was the making of ground-nut oil. Our crop of these nuts being ingathered, I reserved some for seed, and devoted the remainder to the manufacture of oil. The method I adopted (which is that pursued by the Zingas) is as follows:—The ground-nuts are reduced to a kind of coarse flour by pounding them in a mortar. This flour, which is highly oleaginous, is rolled up into large balls, and is in that form exposed to the sun until the oil is seen to distil from the balls, which are then crumbled by very small quantities into a mortar, boiling water being added with each quantity of flour. As the mass increases in the mortar, it is most carefully pressed, and worked with clean peeled sticks. By means of this pressure the oil is separated from the pulp or residuum of flour, which is, of course, disintegrated by the boiling water. The oil being then poured off, the remaining flour is further subjected to a process of wringing in a cloth, by which means yet more oil is extracted. All the oil is then set over the fire in large cooking-pots, and when brought to the boiling-point the heat is abated, and so regulated as to keep the oil at the same temperature for some days. This amount of heat gradually brings all impurities to the surface as a scum, which is carefully removed from time to time until the oil is perfectly clear like the finest olive-oil, which it closely resembles in flavour, or rather, absence of flavour. It is then allowed to cool, and is bottled off for use. In this manner I made about twenty gallons of oil, which was highly appreciated by all who tasted it; but there are other and more frequently adopted methods of extracting it, which result in the manufacture of a very inferior article, that has brought discredit upon ground-nut oil in the world of commerce.

Senhor Carvalho, whose business at Luebo I have omitted to say was canoe-building, had now (Nov. 1886) been some time absent from the station. He had gone to Muansangoma, to procure ivory, with which he returned to Luebo, in order that he might send it down to the coast on board the *Stanley*, which might be coming up at any time. He was also shipping the ivory he had already stored with us, a total altogether of considerably more than one hundred points. While he was away I had, at his request, looked after the canoe-building, which had been so far successful in that he now possessed two really fine canoes of large size, and several smaller. The idea of the partners was to utilise the river down to Kwamouth as a highway by which to carry their merchandise to the riparian tribes. Whether this idea be really practicable or not remained to be proved when I left the district, but my own opinion is, that although the punishments inflicted upon the towns of the predatory Basongo-Meno may have sufficed to make the river safe for the *passage* of any boats or canoes, it is assuming too much to conclude that it must therefore be safe for traders to sojourn amongst the inhabitants, coming and going from town to town, and trafficking, it might be for days at a time, in one place or another. In fact, I am sadly afraid that should he have attempted thus to carry out his plan, all that is mortal of Senhor Antonio Lopes de Carvalho may be now long since assimilated to the baser nature of some sable warrior upon the banks of the Kasaï.

When the *Stanley* at last arrived—in December 1886—she had been long expected. There were on board, besides M. Legât, who was to succeed me at Luebo, Lieut. Taunt, United States Navy, and the Commercial Agent of the State from Léopoldville. Lieut. Taunt was at that time in command of the Sanford expedition, which had been organised by, and largely at the expense of, General Sanford, the United States Minister at Brussels. Its object was to explore the Congo and its tributaries, with the view of acquiring the most reliable and exact statistics that might be obtained as to the commercial capabilities of the vast countries lying within their drainage area, the present state of trade in those regions, and the disposition and nature of the inhabitants. This was a necessary preliminary to the formation of a railway between Mposo and Léopoldville or Kinchasa: a work of supreme importance for the future of the Congo State. My term of service having expired, I was now about to return to Europe. Under some circumstances I would gladly have embraced the opportunity afforded me of encountering new adventures and seeing other countries in the vast basin of the Congo, in furthering the objects of the Sanford expedition; but many signs warned me that my health, which had been wonderfully good throughout the whole period of my life on the Kasaï, required recruiting. So when I had embarked my effects, and taken a somewhat regretful farewell of Senhor Carvalho and many friends amongst the natives—Lieut. Wissmann, who had left Luluaburg for the East Coast on the 16th of November, had written me a most kind adieu on the previous day—I went on board the *Stanley*, and looked my last upon the dark woods and swirling waters of Luebo on the 18th of December 1886.

A few particulars as to our voyage to Léopoldville will bring my narrative of the first ascent of the Kasaï to a conclusion. Nothing of any moment occurred until, on the fourth day after leaving Luebo, we ran upon a snag, which so injured one of the floats of the paddle-wheel that we had to camp at the nearest available island for repairs. This was no great distance above the Basongo-Meno towns burnt by us in the October of the preceding year, and as we had very much less ammunition than we ought to have had, our situation might thus, in an enemy's land, have become somewhat critical. As it happened, however, the wheel was effectually cobbled, and we continued our voyage on the following day without further adventure. Passing the mouth of the Nzali Mpini, we stopped for about half an hour in order to obtain firewood at the island of Kimeh. In our ascent of the river we had not visited this singular spot, which is conspicuous from a considerable distance by reason of its lofty trees. It would appear that for ages this island has been held sacred by the Wabuma as the burial-place of their kings, who lie here interred beneath numerous tumuli and under the ghostly protection of their tutelary fetish. The sepulchral mounds, overshadowed by lofty redwood and similar trees, are formed of well-beaten earth, and are about sixteen feet long, of rather less breadth, and eight feet in height. They are kept fairly free from grass and weeds, and are studded with stones and bits of broken crockery, some choice specimens of the latter being fixed upon poles erected on the mounds. I looked into the fetish-house, and saw many figures of various sizes, male and female, all of them equally hideous and obscene. The island may measure about $2\frac{1}{2}$ miles in length, with a breadth of one mile, and is densely wooded. The only inhabitants we saw were the people who kept the graves, and who had on hand a large stock of firewood, from which they were very glad to sell us a supply at a fair price.

On the eighth day of our voyage we arrived at Kwamouth, where we were most warmly welcomed and hospitably entertained by the Superior and Fathers of the French Mission, to whom the station buildings and enclosures have been handed over. It was intended to establish a new governmental station on the opposite or right bank of the Kwa, and the site had been marked out before our visit : very probably the rapid changes effected by the climate have long since obliterated all traces of anything of the kind. Although only some six months had elapsed since the worthy Fathers had entered into possession, a large number of improvements had been completed in the badly constructed and worse planned station. The water at the landing-place had been deepened, so that steamers could come close inshore, large gardens and plantations had been laid out and brought into cultivation, whose productiveness was testified by an abundant supply of excellent vegetables, including some superb tomatos which the good Fathers kindly gave us. The wretched tumble-down house that stood in the centre of the station had been removed, a new kitchen erected, and all the other buildings thoroughly repaired. The Superior entertained us at luncheon, and I was delighted to meet my former acquaintance, the Abbé Krafft, whom I had last seen at Isanghila. The solitariness of my recent life, broken only by the limited, and occasionally uncongenial company of Europeans, contrasted with the engaging manners, the witty and cultured conversation, the simple but dignified hospitality of the company in which I now found myself, did not fail to impress me deeply; it made me feel already returned and welcomed back to civilisation; while the sacred character of my hosts, no less than their gentle breeding, brought one nearer to the Source from which that civilisation springs. And there is another contrast which always recurs to me whenever I encounter the Fathers of the Catholic Mission in Africa, viz., the enormous difference between missionaries and missionaries, between the highly-born and educated man of great intellectual power, and, it may be, knowledge of the world, who, in a divine enthusiasm for the work, abandons all the prizes that the world can give, and the less than half-educated sectary to whom the mission-field abroad offers a solid advancement from uncertain and ill-paid occupations at home, and who may possibly, if smart enough, turn out a good geographer, but rarely indeed an efficient pioneer of Christianity. The Fathers had built a small house to serve as an oratory, but as yet there was no attempt at a church. I make no doubt, however, but that, when it shall have become a necessity, the church will be there. These men are competent missionaries: personal contact with the people; the going about amongst them doing them physical good; the bettering the general condition of their lives— these things are made to accompany preaching, and to precede theology; and since such was also the method of the First Teacher of Christianity, it is not wonderful that the success of these priests should be sometimes proportionate to their consistency. There is at Kwamouth a large native population within hearing of the mission-bell, and as it daily sings at morn and noon and night the first of all the gospel canticles, we may well hope that ere long it shall not find its only echo in the mighty rivers and the waving woods, but also in the living hearts and lives of men.

We encamped this evening at Ibani, on the south bank of the Congo, and on the following day, the ninth of our voyage, we reached Léopoldville early in the afternoon. At Kinchasa, where we disembarked Lieut. Taunt, we had the pleasure of seeing Mr. Swinburne again; and at Léopoldville we were welcomed by M. Le Marinel, Senior, chief of station; Captain Vangele, administrator of the Upper Congo; M. Steleman, commercial agent; and other Europeans previously known to us.

Thus the record of my experiences in connection with the first attempt to plant civilisation in a vast region of

Central Africa is closed. I trust the narration of circumstances of which, be they great or small, it must be written "*et quorum pars magna fui*," may be helpful to others similarly placed, and of interest to all who have at heart the regeneration of long-degraded races of their fellow-men.

KALLINA POINT.

APPENDIX.

Note A.—*African Servants.*

NEGRO servants, if good, are justly renowned for fidelity and efficiency, and those characteristics are not less marked in their own land than in Europe and America. During my African experiences I had a large number of servants through my hands, of whom the majority gave me satisfaction. Some of the least satisfactory were Christians, and quite the worst, a young fellow known as John Henry, having been trained in Bishop Steere's Mission at Zanzibar, wrote and spoke English perfectly, but was a fearful drunkard, and an accomplished, mischievous, and impudent liar. Of the two servants whom I took with me on the voyage up the Kasaï, the elder, a huge and very ugly Houssa, named Bakari Egba-Ali, a Mohammedan, was the best servant I ever had or ever man need wish to have: truthful, faithful, and ingeniously expert in all things pertaining to personal attendance. I have much cause to feel grateful to him for his unwearied and self-denying attention in health and sickness. Before he came into my service he had been shamefully ill-used by his master, an Englishman, I am sorry to say, but presumably unaccustomed to the command of servants in his native land. Bakari and I parted with mutual regret. The other servant, a lad named Mualo, a native of Lutété, was a faithful creature, a fact proved by his voluntarily offering to accompany me up the Kasaï, at that time a name of ill savour down the Congo.

Note B.—*Central African Scenery and its Critics.*

I have (in the text) below pointedly remarked the occasional beauty and variety of the African forest in the same spirit as I have here admitted (and ascribed to what I believe to be its true cause) that feeling of desolation with which the Congo scenery impresses the beholder. It is pure affectation to pretend that the sunlight in Equatorial Africa is unlike the sunlight in Equatorial anywhere else, or that the magnificent flora which contributes to the glory of many an European hothouse is incapable of endowing with the smallest interest or beauty the land that gives it birth; but! I am sorry to observe that although this affectation is as absurd as its pretensions are false, yet it is nevertheless fashionable. Poor Mr. Smellfungus could never see good in anything except in himself, but then, of course, that was what nobody else could see. Not much happier are such writers in their complaints as to the impoverishing character of the food obtainable in Central Africa: their only ground of plausible excuse being the impossibility of their glutting themselves with vulgar masses of British beef, stodgy potatoes, and bile-creating beer.

NOTE C.—*Forest Trees and Plants.*

Besides the two or three remarkable trees mentioned in the text, there are others almost equally beautiful and of great utility. The bamboos and palms are as well known as they are universally useful. The *Cottonwood* tree is often to be seen towering above the rest of the forest to a height little short of 200 feet. It is deciduous, and is noticeable both for its immense height, the curious buttress-like supports which grow up from its roots on all sides, and its smooth slate-grey coloured trunk rising branchless almost to the point at which the umbrella-like crown terminates its upward growth. The wood of this tree is perfectly white, very soft, and, when seasoned, as light as cork. It is used for a variety of purposes, and out of the flat slabs obtained from the buttresses the natives form platters and dishes. The *Kusu-kusu*—another lofty, straight, and branchless tree—is much used for "dug-out" canoes. The leaves are leathery, dark, and evergreen. The water-loving *Redwood* also occasionally attains a great height, although its habit of growth is somewhat spreading. Its foliage, which is very dark and glossy, grows in dense and handsome masses. Very similar is the *Camwood*, from which the red powder of native commerce is obtained. The *Teak* tree must be reckoned amongst the larger timber trees, and is common enough: tall and straight, with dark, glossy foliage, decidedly handsome. The *Sàkabu* is also a lofty tree, often growing to a height of from 100 to 150 feet. In form and outline it much resembles the silver fir, though its foliage is of course—for it is not a conifer—utterly dissimilar. The bark is rough, and brown in colour; the branches leave the trunk almost at right angles; and the leaves, dark hued and lanceolate, are evergreen. This tree is chiefly valued on account of its resinous exudations, which are used in the manufacture of torches, known on the coast as "bush candles." The *Baobab*, another forest giant, is, in my opinion, unsightly, although it has many admirers. Its most striking peculiarity is the position of the fruit, which hang singly on long caudicles—I lack a more exact word—from two to six feet from the parent stem, precisely, of course, where the blossoms have been. It is always grotesquely branched, and differently in different specimens; some possessing great undivided trunks, and others branching almost from the ground. There are no twigs properly so called—only small but comparatively thick branchlets, from which the leaves and the long flower-stems grow. The bark, which is quite smooth and somewhat glossy, is grey in colour, and the evergreen foliage, which is very sparse, is light green. The blossom is large, something like an enormously exaggerated myrtle flower, and of a greenish white colour. The fruit is a curious gourd-like globe, with a velvety surface, at first green, but ripening into brown. In size the fruit varies from a diameter of four inches to one of eight. On being opened, a fibrous brush-like lining to the shell is laid bare, which is utilised for brushes and scrubbers. The wood is worthless, but Senhor Monteiro, believing that excellent paper could be manufactured from this tree, experimented successfully with the inner bark, and eventually established a small mill with suitable machinery for the manufacture at Maculla on the west coast, north of Ambrizette. The natives, however, judged that Senhor Monteiro and his machinery were weaving charms and a diabolical fetish against them, and they accordingly soon made an end of the whole concern by smashing up and destroying the mill and its contents. Amongst less lofty trees we have the *acacias* already named, with flowers pink, white, and

M

yellow; feathery *mimosas;* the *ebony* tree, the *Arbor vitæ,* and many others the names of which I do not know. Two of the most noteworthy of the trees of moderate height are the *bush mangrove* and the *Banyàn or Saffu.* The former is chiefly remarkable for resemblance to its salt-marsh kinsman, from which, however, it differs in that it is a deciduous tree, and lacks those peculiarities which make its relative a harbourer of pestilence. The *Saffu,* a most umbrageous tree, is always planted by the natives in their towns, where its shade affords a convenient shelter for the village conclave. The fruit, closely resembling in appearance a magnum-bonum plum, though larger, is very acid. As an article of food it is best roasted on the wood ashes, and so roasted is frequently made up into a very agreeable confection with sugar and cream. There are two remarkable trees very commonly to be met with bearing quantities of fruit which, although of large size and tempting appearance, are useless for food, whatever their medicinal qualities may or may not be. The *Elephant-apple* or *Jack-fruit* tree is a denizen of the woodlands, where it grows to a considerable size in moist soils. The apple, as it is called, is considerably larger than the average unhusked cocoa-nut, and when ripe is a gorgeous-looking fruit, bearing all shades of yellow, from a pale lemon colour to the most brilliant orange. Its outer skin is marked and embossed in small hexagonal compartments, which, on an attempt being made to tear them off, are found to continue through to the centre of the fruit, precisely like the sections of a fir cone. As an article of food, however, this superb-looking fruit is utterly disappointing, being slightly sweet indeed, but very dry, and redolent of turpentine. The natives use it for "medicine." The utmost praise I can bestow upon it is to say that I believe it is not poisonous. The other wild fruit tree that I allude to is called "*Zilu*" by the natives, and is to be found everywhere on the grassy plains and old clearings in the neighbourhood of villages. It is a low-growing, round-topped tree, with rather bright evergreen leaves. The blossom is white and star-shaped, but uninteresting. The fruit, quite globular in shape and smooth skinned, of the size of a large orange, is remarkable for the changes its colour undergoes in the process of ripening: green, lead-colour, and finally orange. The rind is extremely thick, and almost as tough as wood.

APPENDIX.

The interior contains a yellow pulp, very sweet, but painfully astringent. The natives employ it as "medicine," but not for food. Lieut. Wissmann ate two of these fruits, and in consequence suffered a good deal from nausea. He stated that the fruit contains strychnia, and I believe that it is slightly poisonous. Throughout the forest multitudes of creeping plants and trees are to be found, notably the indiarubber vine (not the small-leaved *Ficus repens* of our English hothouses), the creeping bamboo, the orchilla weed, and many other parasites, as ferns and orchids, which drape the greater stems and weave the lesser trees into an impenetrable screen, or bring fresh light and beauty into many a shady place. There are a multitude of shrubs, many of them of great beauty, curious plants, ferns, and mosses, some known indeed to botanists and collectors, but many more, I am persuaded, still awaiting discovery and classification.

Note D.—*The Kwango.*

The upper part of the river Kwango was thoroughly explored in 1883 by Major Mechow, who descended the river until within 100 miles of the Kwa, where farther navigation downward was stopped by the very considerable falls to which that explorer has given his name. Subsequently Lieut. Massari ascended the Kwango until within a short distance of Mechow Falls, but he had to return owing to lack of provisions. The river is about 900 miles long, and deep, but swift and narrow. For long portions of its course it is navigable, but not continuously. It drains a large area lying at a much higher elevation than that of the Kasaï, into which stream it falls at 3° 17′ 30″ S., 17° 45′ E.

Note E.—*The Lukenyé.*

It is as yet (March 1888) uncertain where the Lukenyé debouches. That there is such a river the reports of Portuguese traders, and the partial exploration by Lieut. Kund of the Berlin African Exploration Society, sufficiently demonstrate. If it joins the Kasaï at all as an independent stream—and I believe that I am justified in saying that Lieut. Kund is of opinion that it does—it must join it at this point (Mount Poggé) and at none other. It is just possible, however, that the river which Mr. Stanley observed issuing into the Nzali Mpini on its left bank shortly before he discovered Lake Léopold II., and which in his chart he would identify with the Kasaï—the magnitude of which stream he must have underrated enormously—is the Lukenyé. But there is more than one curious point connected with Lake Léopold II. which from its discovery has remained unsolved, and I should not be surprised if by far the greater portion of what its discoverer calls its southern (really eastern) shore should prove to be a vast island contained between the lake and a lacustrine river leaving it where Mr. Stanley notes "submerged forest" or "submerged land," and coming out into the Nzali Mpini, where I have remarked that it may be barely possible that the Lukenyé discharges its waters.

Note F.—*Basongo Meno.*

In employing this designation for the wild tribes upon the Kasaï, I must explain that I am perfectly well aware that there is no people or nation to whom the term specially applies, and that the term itself (of Bakongo origin) simply describes a people with filed or broken teeth: in point of fact, the designation has been used for tribes otherwise very dissimilar and inhabiting the Aruwhimi region. I use it *faute de mieux* because others use it, and because it is convenient to have some general term for those nearly related tribes inhabiting the banks of the Middle Kasaï, and who, however much they may differ from each other, differ still more from their Wabuma and Bayanzi neighbours on the one hand, and the Bakuba, Shammatuka, and Bakètè on the other. As a matter of fact, we know very little about them indeed, and despite the pretentious divisions and nomenclature of the recently published Gotha map, we can know but very little about them for an indefinite period to come. They certainly are not kin to the Bangalas of the Congo, though I myself hold that they are closely connected, if not identical, with the Tucongo, and have consequently a southeastern origin. If anybody knows anything at all about these people, it is Dr. Wolf, who has, I believe, a theory of his own upon the subject—a theory, however, with which I am not acquainted. As to the names and allotments of these tribes and districts as given in the map above referred to, all I can say is that they are nearly all Ki-Swahili names, manifestly given by Zanzibaris to inquiring geographers either in description or derision of the people to whom they are applied; *e.g.*, "Muana Makima" = *Sons of monkeys;* "Ben-ngonde" = *Moonstruck folk*. It should be remembered that however much akin Ki-Swahili is to some languages of Congoland, it has no practical connection whatever with those of the Basongo Meno, Tu Congo, or Shammatuka tribes.

NOTE G.—*Vermin and Household Pests.*

The mosquitos that emanated from the lagoon at Luebo were a serious annoyance in the station, as were also swarms of midges. We were plagued with multitudes of house-flies, and the common mangrove fly, a blood relation to the horse-fly or clegg of our northern British moors, was numerous. There were a few tarantula spiders, scorpions both black and grey, chiefly the latter, centipedes, though rare, hornets of three different kinds, and a species of wasp building in the houses. In the station itself there were no white ants, though there was an abundance of them close at hand, and we rarely had any snakes inside our palisades: mice and rats were also uncommon. We had no chigoes—the chigger of the West Indies—but doubtless they are by this time introduced at Luebo, along with civilisation, from the coast. It is said that they die out in places which they have infested for twenty years.

NOTE H.—*Lhiamba Song.*

The song most commonly sung during the lhiamba smoking at nights in the Lubuku towns is a short and extremely simple melody, taken up indiscriminately by men and women, some singing the air, while others sustain a rude harmony or beat time on the tom-toms. Occasionally it seemed to me that (doubtless by accident) the voices were singing the melody in canon. Subsequently, on writing it down,

182   APPENDIX.

I saw that my ear had not deceived me: the repeat occurs in the sixth bar. It may be noted as follows:—

Its performance takes place after the Kinsu has made one or two rounds, and is prefaced by a prelude of drumming in strict time on the tom-toms (ndunga). A man starts up and delivers in wild recitative a rhythmical verse or verses upon topical subjects of the day. The verse is destitute of rhyme—I question much whether the Bashilangé have any idea of rhyme—and is delivered in monotone to the accompaniment of the tom-toms. At a point in their recitative the chorus break in, the women generally leading off, and the refrain is repeated and kept up for a longer or shorter period;—the words being pure rubbish. Those given above simply mean, " Welcome, brethren, welcome heartily; with us all men are kin." Then another reciter stands forth probably less coherent in his utterances than the former, and the performance is repeated and repeated, together with the concomitant smoking, coughing, and screeching, literally *usque ad nauseam*. I ought to observe that in the above "score" the second part is written in the bass clef for convenience of distinction merely.

NOTE J.—*Lubuku*.

Lubuku may be described as a secret society or organisation of which the Bashilangé-Baluba king is *ex officio* the head, but it is primarily a social organisation, and only indirectly of political importance. I call it a secret society, not only because its rules, regulations, signs, and working are secret, but because the very aims and objects of its existence are unknown to outsiders, while its initiatory rites have never (despite many pretences to the contrary) been witnessed by an uninitiated person or revealed to an European. Certain external evidences of its inward nature are, however, sufficiently obvious to all who care to investigate the subject. One thing it does not effect, and that is anything tangible in the way of philanthropy. On the contrary, the lhiamba smoking which it encourages has a most disastrous effect on both the health and wealth of its devotees and the villages they inhabit. A dark inference as to its true nature may be drawn from the lax, and, indeed, promiscuous intercourse which it promotes between the sexes, for although Lubuku does not profess to interfere with marriage as an institution, yet by its establishing a community of wives (and consequently of husbands, for the sexes are treated on an equality) amongst its members, it saps the very foundations of social propriety. Another indication of its licentious nature is afforded by the customs observed at the marriages of its male members, and repeated for three successive nights, in which all decency is outraged in the most revolting and most public way imaginable. The initiatory rites of the society are performed generally by the King or by Meta Sankolla on an islet in the Lulua a short distance above Luluaburg, but, as I have observed above, what those rites may be nobody knows. There are no funereal ceremonies observed at the death or burial of a member of this fraternity, but it is to be remembered that obsequies of any kind are unknown amongst the Bashilangé, although, in common with most African races, and unlike the Basongo Meno, who *utilise* the bodies of departing relatives, they bury their dead with all requisite decency.

NOTE K.—*Temperature, &c., during the Wet and Dry Seasons at Luebo.*

AVERAGE OF BAROMETER READINGS AT LUEBO.

Barometer (Holosterie) Station, 1650 feet over sea-level.

MONTH.	7 A.M.	2 P.M.	9 P.M.
July (dry) . August (dry) .	734.25	735.0	734.75
October (wet) . November (wet) .	734.5	733.25	732.75

THERMOMETER READINGS AT LUEBO.

Centigrade Thermometers by Greiner & Son, Berlin.

MONTH.	7 A.M.	2 P.M.	9 P.M.
July . August .	19.5	30.5	23.5
October . November .	22.5	36.5	25.5

Highest point reached in months { July . . 35.5
                                        { October . . 40.5
Lowest point reached in months { July . . 17.5
                                        { October . . 21.75
Prevailing winds during the day (dry season) . S.S.E. & S. ½ E.
        ,,   ,,   ,, (wet season) . S.E. & E.S.E.
        ,,   ,, night (dry season) . N.N.W. & N. ½ E.
        ,,   ,,   ,, (wet season) . W.N.W. & W. ½ N.

The rainy season begins about the second week in September, and continues variably until the third week of April. Heavy rains commence in November, and last about six weeks, being accompanied by severe thunderstorms and tornados. The rivers are at their highest level in March, and lowest in August. Altogether the climate is extremely damp, and had it not been for the excellent air-tight uniform-cases supplied to me by Messrs. Silver of Cornhill (whose travellers' and explorers' requisites I can thoroughly recommend), not only would all my papers have perished, but I should have been destitute of clothing long before my term of service at Luebo had expired.

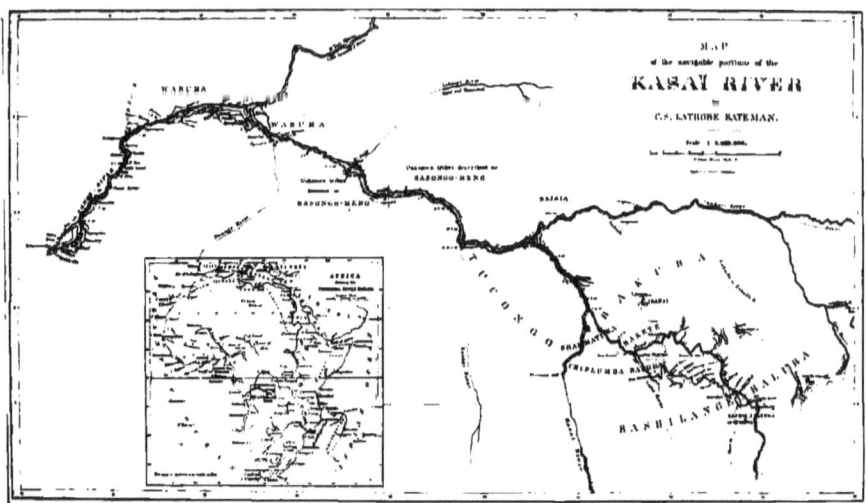

INDEX.

A.

ACACIAS, 13, 132, and Appendix C.
African servants, Appendix A.
Alligators, 59, 79, 155.
Ambakistas, 125.
Ambrizette, Appendix C.
Andersson, Lieut., 4, 52, 103.
Angelus, the, at Kwamouth, 173.
Angola, 2, 46, 163.
Angolese, *vide En Avant* crew, and 125.
Ant-bear, 155.
Antelopes, 13, 154, 155.
Ants, 155.
Apes, 132, 155.
Aquatic birds, 53, 59.
Arabs, 94.
Arachis, *vide* Ground-nut.
Arms (Basongo-Meno), 41.
Arts, 34, 73.

B.

BAILUNDA, 22, 23, 82.
Bakari, Appendix A.
Bakètó, 19, 22, 23.
—— chiefs as allies, 145.
—— described, 68.
—— industries, 69-73.
—— hunting, 152, 153.
—— hunters, accident to, 149, 150.
—— plantations, 68.
Bakuba, 21, 22, 54.
—— cloth, 21.
—— fishermen, 56.
—— head-dress, 54.
—— misunderstanding with, 142 146.
Bakwengi Babiaha, 22, 57.
Baluba, 19.
—— and Bakuba, an incident, 55.
—— Bashilangé, 19, 20.
—— Chiplumba, 63, 64, 105.
Balungu, 23, 123, 124.
Bambangala, 154.
Bamboo (creeping), 13, 131.
Banana, 101.
Bananas, 16, 34, 45, 147.
Banyàn, 69, and Appendix C.
Baobab, 5, and Appendix C.
Bashilangé, *vide* Baluba.
Basongo-Meno, 17, 39, and Appendix F.
—— arts and utensils, 40.
—— houses, 37, 41.
—— language not understood by interpreters or by Baluba, 42.
—— women and youth, 42.
Batèké, 8.
Bats, 25, 132, 149, 153.
Batua Bankonko, 23, 68, 85, 145.
Batua Basinji, 23.
Bayanzi, 24.
—— canoe incident, 8.
Beans, 142.
Beetroot, 142.
Bellows, curious Basongo-Meno, 44.
Benguela, 78.
Beni Kashia, 64, 105, 134-137.
Beni Muamba, 106, 128-130.
Beni Ndumba, 126, 127.
Bibòkó, 27, 28.
Bihanos, 156, 157.
Bihé, 157.
Bimba, 166.
Biombé, 64, 164-167.
Bittern, 132.
Bombax, 2, and Appendix C.
Boa-constrictor, 155.
Borassus palm, 45.
Bosjie-Massari, 31, 32.
Buffaloes, 38, 131, 132, 153, 154.
Bugslag, Herr, 2, 107, 109, 121.
Bull-frogs, 133.
Bullock, an eccentric, 108.
Burning brandy, an incident, 120.
Bush-pig, 155.

C.

CABBAGE, 69, 142.
Calemba, 2, 4, 67, 112, 115-119, 164, 165, and Appendix J.

Cameron, Commander, R.N., 69 (footnote), 78, 124, 157.
Camwood, Appendix C.
Camp above laterite cliffs (16th Oct.), 34.
—— at Beni-Kashia, 105, 134–137.
—— at Beni-Muamba, 129, 130.
—— at Bosjie-Massari, 31.
—— at Chinyama, 107.
—— at Chitabo on Miaw, 107.
—— at deserted fishing-village on Lulua, 59–60.
—— at deserted town beyond Beni Muamba, 106.
—— at deserted town beyond Musisi, 106.
—— at deserted Wabuma fishing-town, 25.
—— at Gates of the Pool, 5.
—— at Ibani, 173.
—— at Luangi mouth, 45, 46.
—— at last borassus palm, 45.
—— at Mallagóhònó, 28.
—— at Mbembo, 25.
—— at Musshwa (scene of wreck), 7–9.
—— at Nganebecca, 30.
—— at Sankoro mouth, 49–53.
—— near deserted village (17th Oct.), 35.
—— on island (22nd Oct.), 39.
—— on island (23rd, 24th, and 25th Oct.), 39–43.
—— on island (2nd Nov.), 54.
—— on Nov. 3rd, 55.
—— on Nov. 4th, 56.
—— on Oct. 18th, 35.
—— on Oct. 19th and 20th, 35, 36.
—— on Oct. 26th, 44.
—— on sandbank in Lulua, 57, 58.
—— opposite Macan, 11.
—— opposite Maliva, 11–13.
—— opposite Mount Poggé, 36, 37.
Canoe-building, Senhor Carvalho's, 168.
Canoes destroyed, 44.
Cape hunting-dog, 154.
Carvalho, Senhor A. L. de, history &c., 81–86, 88, 89, 103, 142, 143.
—— in charge of Luebo, 139, 140, 160.
—— letter, 86–88.
—— parting with, 170.
—— trade prospects, 168, 169.
Cassava, *vide* Manioc.
Castellated rocks, 27.
Caxavalla, Silva da Costa, Senhor Manoel, 120–123.
Celery, 142.
Chienvu, 159.
Chigoes, Appendix G.
Chikabo, 105, 135–137, 160, 164.
Chikumba, 51.

Chilunga Meso, 116–124, 159.
Chinyama, 107.
Chipaka, 51.
Chiplumba tribes and country, 63, 64.
Chissèngenéné, 72.
Christmas festivities, 75, 76.
Chitabo, 107.
Cicada, 132.
Civets, 154.
Comber, Rev. T. J., 29 (footnote).
Congolemosch, 111, 115, 159.
Congo Manena, 19, 58, 67.
Cottonwood tree, 97, and Appendix C.
Cotton, 142.
Courts-martial, 77.
Cowbirds, 38.
Custodio, Senr., *vide* Souza-Machado.

D.

DANCING, 75, 76.
Darling, Rev. F. C., 29 (footnote).
Debinga Debeha, 161–163.
Descent of Kasaï, *vide* Wissmann, Lieut.
Dogs, Bakètè, 73, 152, 153.
Domingos, Jaô, 160–163.
"Dover Cliffs," 5.
Draining (plantations), 141.

E.

EAGLES, 155.
Earth-pig, "Ardvaak," 155.
Egyptian geese, 53, 155.
Eland, 36, 155.
Elephant-apple, Appendix C.
Elephants, 95, 154.
En Avant aground, 55.
—— crew, 3.
—— disabled, 100.
—— late, 45, 57.
—— on Sankoro, 93.
—— wrecked, 5, 6.

F.

FALLS, Luebo, 101, 103, 104, 138, 149–152.
—— Lulua, 17, 61.
—— Wissmann, 104.
Farinha de manioc, 72.
Fetishes at cross-roads, 114, 115 (footnote).
—— at Kimeh, 171.

INDEX. 189

Fetishism, 20, 21, 114, 115.
Fireworks, 146.
Fish (Lulua), 59.
Fish-eagles, 59.
Fishermen, *vide* Bakuba.
Forest, description of the, 12, 13, and Appendix C.
Forest, camp in the, 131-133.

G.

GAME, 13, 36, 132, 133, 154, 155.
Gankabé, 27.
Gates of the Pool, 5.
Goat-sucker, 132.
Gomez, 108.
Gourds, 142.
Grazing land, 127, 128.
Grenadilhas, 142.
Grenfell, Rev. G., 100.
Greshoff, Meinheer, 100.
Ground-nut, 68, 142.
—— oil, 167, 168.
Guinea-fowl, 155.

H.

"HARNESS-back" antelope, 109, 155.
Heronry at fishing-town, 25.
Hippopotami, 35.
Hippopotamus collides with *Stanley*, 56.
—— traps, 53.
Hospitalities, official, 77.
Howitzer, 92.
Humba, 40, 93.
Hunters, *vide* Bakété.
Hunting, *vide* Bakété.
Huts at Shammatuka fishing-town, 60.
Hyenas, 133, 154.

I.

IBIS, 155.
Ichneumon, 154, 155.
Iguana, 155.
Interpreter, importance of office of, 121.
Iron, native, how obtained, 35.
Ivory, trade in, 83-85.
—— transmission of, 88, 168.
—— value of, 85.

J.

JACKALS, 133, 154.
Janssen, Lieut., 13.
Jungle-cock, 131.
Jungle-rat, 155.

K.

KABÃO, 85, 86.
Kabèmbé, 162.
Kafinga, 79, 80.
Kalambaï town, 127.
—— stream, 127.
—— valley, 126.
Kalonda, 164-167.
Kampoto, 70.
Kappasiero, 75.
Kapuku or Muansangoma, 81, 85, 88, 168.
Kasaï, abortive attempt to explore Upper, 100.
—— contrasted with Sankoro, 50-52.
—— exploration above confluence with Lulua, 50, 51, 102.
—— results of exploration, 104.
Kashia-Calemba, 110, 112.
Kasongo, 123, 124, 164.
Kassava, *vide* Manioc.
Kassèngé, 68, 69, 145.
Kimeh island, 170-171.
Kimpoko, 5.
Kinchasa, 3-5, 173.
Kinsu dhiamba, 106, 113.
Kokóró, 28.
Krafft, Mons. l'Abbé, 172.
Kudu, 155.
Kund, Lieut., Appendix E.
Kusu-kusu, Appendix C.
Kwa or Kwamuni, 1, 24, 25.
Kwamouth, 15, 16, 171-173.
Kwango, 30, 33, and Appendix D.

L.

LAKOMBI, 87.
Landslip at Beni-Kashia, 105.
—— at Beni-Muamba, 128.
—— near Ndumba, 128.
Legát, Mons., 169.
Le Marinel, Lieut., 103, 105, 164.
Leopards, 154.
Léopold II., Lake, 27, and Appendix E.
Léopoldville, 2, 4, 173.
Lettuce, 142.
Leslie, Dr., 9, 25, 66.
Lhiamba (*Cannabis Indica*), 40.
—— smoking, 113 114.
—— song, Appendix H.
Limo, 130, 136.
Livingstone, Dr., 1, 83.
Lizards, 155.
Loanda, 84.
Log-hut, 66, 67.

Lomami, 51, 94.
Lombali, 51.
Luangi, 45, 46, 84.
Lubi, 51.
Lubiranzi, 1, 95.
Lubuiju, 86.
Lubuku, 106, 112, 114, 115, and Appendix J.
Luburi or Lubudi, 51, 86.
Luebo Falls, 101, 103, 104, 138, 151, 152.
—— fortifications finished, 147.
—— plantations, 141. 142, 147.
—— river, 2, 51, 58, 61.
—— station, 91, 92.
—— storehouse built, 74.
Luisi, 106, 130.
Lukash, 51.
Lukenyé, 36, and Appendix E.
Lukenga Manena, 158, 160.
Lukwengo, 21, 22.
Lulua, 2, 17, 20, 22, 51, 58.
—— Falls, 61.
—— fish, 59.
—— survey, 143, 144, 147-148.
Lulnaburg, 2, 64, 109, 110, 125, 162, 163, 164, 165.

M.

MÁCAR, Monseigneur le Baron de, 103, 105, 163.
Magic, belief in, 80, 115, 136, 150, 151.
Magnolia, 13.
Malange, 2, 83, 84.
Mallagohònó, 28.
Mangangas, 69, 109.
Mangrove bush, Appendix C.
Manioc, 68, 70-72.
Manoel and the candle, an incident, 45.
Matchioko, characteristics of, 22, 23, 84, 112, 115.
—— intrigues of, 164, 165.
Matjambo, 22, 82, 83.
Mbaku, 132, 154.
Mbembo, 25.
Meta Sankolla, 112, and Appendix J.
Metempsychosis, 159.
Miaw, 51, 107, 125, 126.
Mimosas, Appendix C.
Mirambo, 94.
Mission, American Methodist, 5.
—— Baptist, 101.
—— Catholic, 171-173.
Mpinda Nguba, vide Ground-nut.
Mpondo, vide Sorghum.
Moèro, Lake, 83.
Mohamadi, 145, 166.
Monteiro, Senr., Appendix C.

Mosquitos, Appendix G.
Msuata, 13.
Mtama, vide Sorghum.
Mualo, Appendix A.
Muanamput, 107.
Muansangoma, 51, 81, 84, 88, 102.
Muata Nzigé, 102.
Mukanu, 129.
Muléo, 24.
Mummy-pea, 69 (footnote).
Musisi, 106, 128, 130, 133.
Musjie, 27.

N.

NGANEBECCA, 30.
Ngombé Ngollé, vide Bambangala.
Niapara, vide Mohamadi.
Night in the forest, 131-133.
Night on the Kasaï, 47, 48.
Nimptsch, Herr Baron von, 100.
Nkaka, 59.
Nkulé, 30.
Nyamwezu, 94.
Nzali Mpini, 1, 27, 33, 104, and Appendix E.

O.

OKRAS, 142.
Olsen, Mr., 4, 35, 40, 42.
Onças, 154.
Onions, 127, 142.
Orchilla, 132, and Appendix C.
Orchids, Appendix C.
Otters, 154.

P.

PALM-WINE, 45, 57 (footnote).
Panther, 154.
Paper-making, Appendix C.
Parrot, King, 98.
—— Mr. Vander Felson's, 10, 11.
Parrots, wild, 155.
Partridge, 155.
Pavilion at Luebo (how built), 91-92.
Pea-nut, vide Ground-nut.
Peace, SS., 100, 102, 104.
Pigeons, 155.
Pine-apples, 142.
Pioko, 109.
Pipe-clay, 74 (footnote).
Plantain-eaters, 155.
Plantains, 37, 147.
Plantations, Kassèngé, 68, 69, 101
—— Luebo, 140-142.

INDEX.

Plantations, Luluaburg, 110.
Poggé, Dr., 1, 83, 84.
—— Expedition, 1.
—— Mount, 36, 37, and Appendix E.
Ponde, vide Sorghum.
Porcupine, 155.
Potatoes, sweet, 68.

Q.

QUAIL, 155.
Queens, Wabuuna, 27.
—— Zinga, 91.

R.

RAPIDS, vide Falls.
Rats, 59, 155.
Redwood, Appendix C.
Roadmaking, 92, 147.
Route survey (Luluaburg to Luebo), 125–138.
Routine, daily, 76, 77.
Royal, SS., 9.

S.

SAFFU, vide Banyan.
Salt, how extracted, 72.
Sanford Expedition, 169, 170.
—— General, 169.
Sankoro contrasted with Kasaï, 51, 52.
—— explored, 93–95.
—— mouth, 51.
Sappoo Sahib, 94.
Saturnino, Senhor, vide Souza-Machado.
Saulez, Captain, 2.
Scenery on Congo, 13, and Appendix B.
Schneider, Mr., 4, 45, 65, 67, 79, 93 (footnote).
Schwerin, Monseigneur le Baron de, 103, 104.
Shammatuka, 22, 57, 59–60, 64.
Sibissi, 155.
Slaves, trading in, 84, 85, 157.
Snakes, 155.
Songo Nzadi, 59.
Sorghum, 142.
Souza-Machado, Senhor Custodio, 82–84.
—— Senhor Saturnino, 81, 84, 86, 88–90, 102.
Spear-grass, 128.
Spur-winged plover, 133.
Squirrel, species of, 155.
Stanley, Mr. H. M., 1, 13, and Appendix E.
Stanley Pool, 4, 5, 173.
Stanley, SS., accident to, in descending Kasaï, 170.

Stanley, SS., passes En Avant, 9.
—— incidents during ascent of Kasaï, 39, 42, 45, 47, 49, 55, 56.
—— leaves Luebo, 65.
—— returns to Luebo and departs, 103, 105.
—— returns again in December, 169.
—— crew and passengers, 4.
Storehouse, how built, 73, 74.
Sukabu, Appendix C.
Sunday, how observed, 78.
Surprises, agreeable, 96, 97.
Swinburne, Mr., 9, 173.

T.

TANGANYKA, 124.
Taunt, Lieut., 169, 173.
Teak-tree, Appendix C.
Theft on board Stanley, 55.
Thunderstorm at Beni-Kashia, an incident, 135, 136.
Tippoo Tib, 94.
Tobacco, 69. 70.
Tomatos, 142, 172.
Tortoise, 155.
Toucans, 155.
Trade prospects of riverine, 169.
—— expedition, 169, 170.
Travellers'-tree, 13.
Tributaries of Kasaï and Sankoro, 51.
Troup, Mr. J. R., 2, 9.
Tsétsé 128.
Tucongo, 22, 84.
Turnips, 142.

U.

ULUNGU, 124. 164.
Urnki or Burnki, 1, 95.
Utensils, Bakètè, 72.
—— Basongo-Meno, 40.

V.

VALLEY, Luebo, 105.
—— Musisi, 106.
Vangele, Captain, 173.
Vander Felson, Mr., 3.
—— affects sandbanks, 55, 56.
—— at Luebo, 65, 67.
—— farewell and death, 101.
—— goes with Dr. Wolf to the Sankoro, 79.
—— ill with fever, 35.
—— leaves with Dr. Wolf for Kasaï, 100.

INDEX.

Vander Felson, loses his parrot, 10.
—— recovers his health, 45.
—— recriminative, 7.
—— returns with many parrots, 97-98.
—— taken down to Leopoldville in the *Peace*, 101.
Vermin, 155, and Appendix G.

W.

WAAL, Mr., 4.
Wabuma fishing-town, 25, 26.
Waders, 59, 155.
Walker, Mr., 3, 7, 9, 10, 11, 65.
War-scare, 145, 146.
Water or reed buck, 155.
Waterhen, 155.
Whaleboat, 17, 37, 39, 52, 100.
—— refitted, 102.
Whitewash, 74, and footnote.
Wild duck, 53, 155.
Winton, Sir Francis de, K.C.M.G., 4, 9.
Wissmann Falls, 104.
Wissmann, Lieut., 1, 2, and Appendix C.
—— accident at the Pioko, 109.
—— discovery and descent of Kasaï, 17-19.
—— expedition referred to, 39, 44, 111.
—— explores Kasaï above confluence with Lulua, 104, 105.
—— goes to Luluaburg with Dr. Wolf, 102.
—— native name given to, 159.
—— receives embassy from Ulungu, 124.
—— receives Congolemosch's homage, 111, 112.
—— returns from Madeira, 100.
—— returns to Luebo *viâ* Muansangoma, 102.
—— sets out for Ulungu, 164.
—— starts for east coast (16/11/86), 170.

Wissmann, Lieut., starts for Luluaburg, 105.
—— visits Calemba, 112.
—— visited by Chilunga Meso, 117, 118.
Witchcraft, *vide* Magic.
Wolf, Herr Dr., 2, 4, 65, and Appendix F.
—— at Sankoro mouth, 52.
—— at scene of *En Avant's* wreck, 9.
—— at Wabuma heronry, 25.
—— designs the log-house, 66.
—— goes to Luluaburg, 67.
—— goes to Luluaburg with Wissmann, 102.
—— his exploration of Sankoro summarised, 95.
—— in Basongo-Meno country, 36-39, 42.
—— leaves in *En Avant* for the Sankoro, 79.
—— leaves again to explore Kasaï, 99-100.
—— leaves on board *Stanley* for Europe, 105.
—— returns for the New Year, 78.
—— returns to Luebo, 100.
—— returns to Luebo, and leaves with Wissmann to explore Kasaï, 102.
—— returns to Luebo, 104.
—— returns on board the *Peace*, 101.
Wooding, 28, 29.
Wreck, *vide En Avant*.

Y.

YAM, wild, how prepared, 70.

Z.

ZANZIBAR, 102.
Zanzibaris, *vide En Avant* crew.
Zingas 89 91.

www.ingramcontent.com/pod-product-compliance
Lightning Source LLC
Chambersburg PA
CBHW031738230426
43669CB00007B/395